twelve tips to
RESOLVING
STRESS
in Your Marriage

How to identify and solve the twelve most common problems that produce stress and hinder intimacy in marriage.

twelve tips to
RESOLVING
STRESS
in Your Marriage

How to identify and solve the twelve most common
problems that produce stress and hinder intimacy in marriage

© 2003, 2004, 2005 Jimmy Evans
ISBN # 1-931585-09-1

Cover design by Cenveo, Amarillo, Texas

MARRIAGETODAY™
P.O. Box 8400
Amarillo, TX 79114
1-866-800-3244
www.marriagetoday.org

10 9 8 7 6 5 4 3 2

Dedication

I dedicate this book to my parents, M.L. and Mary Evans. Their example of godly character and commitment to marriage and family has had a deep impact upon my life. I have watched as they have gone through the most stressful and difficult circumstances one can imagine. However, regardless of the size of the challenges they have faced, they have faced them together and always found a way to learn from adversity and come out better on the other side. They are living examples of the power of commitment and what God can do through people who will not give up on Him or each other. I am thankful to have them as my parents.

Acknowledgments

There are many people who have influenced the writing of this book from beginning to end. I have the greatest staff in the world to work with every day. Their encouragement, editing skills and hard work have been invaluable. I would like to thank Tom Lane, Byron Gossett, Donna Griffin, Kelli Bullard, Kim LaNore, Kimberly Fritts and Tanya Spivey. I extend a special thanks to Steve Trafton and the staff of Cenveo-Trafton. And, as always, I thank the Board of Directors of Family & Marriage Today™ for their constant supply of wisdom and encouragement.

Last, but not least, I thank the very important people God has put around me to support everything I do. My wife, Karen, is an integral part of everything in my life. Without her Christ-like love and faithful prayers for me, this book wouldn't have happened. Bo Williams and the incredible staff and elder body of Trinity Fellowship Church are blessings in my life beyond description. I can write books like this because of their willingness to diligently care for the flock.

Table of Contents

Introduction

More than 100 years ago, a powerful momentum began that has forever changed the lives of mankind. It began with the Industrial Age, swept through the turn of the 20th Century, barreled through two world wars, was attacked socially in the 60s, and then picked up more speed in the last 25 years than ever before, forever changing the way we live.

That momentum—which drives our daily lives—is stress.

That momentum – which drives our daily lives – is stress.

When the Industrial Age began, the world was an agrarian society. Life had a very slow pace.

But today, more than a century later and with the technological age, we are a driven culture.

We rise early to beat the rush hour traffic, race to get our children to school, and fly across the country and back in a single day for business meetings. Our families are two-income households juggling careers, parenting, marriage and housework. We schedule appointments for everything—play dates, soccer practice, therapy, car repairs, and even the dog's grooming.

It's a far cry from the days of country life—rising with the sun with only one major task on the agenda, and then going to bed at sunset after a hard day's work. It's a far cry from the one-room schoolhouse.

So how have we fared?

Not too well.

The stress of our driven culture has taken its toll. Its excessiveness has devastated our physical, mental and emotional health. Unhealthy stress has reached epidemic proportions— and nowhere has it been felt more than in our marriages.

Couples today have to fight to stay married. While a hundred years ago, splitting up wasn't even seriously considered, today it's easier to divorce than to try to resolve all of the conflict created by the excessive stress.

But despite all of this negative pressure, maintaining a loving and flourishing marriage is not impossible.

God has solutions. His Word is filled with practical wisdom and godly advice—and so is this book.

Drawing from more than 20 years of counseling married couples and families in crisis, I have seen the patterns of what stress can do to unravel lives. And I have found God's answers to resolving the many stress-filled circumstances of marriage...

- money and financial problems
- sexual issues
- the heartbreak of divorce
- adjusting to remarriage and the blended family
- physical abuse
- dealing with in-laws
- agreeing on disciplining the children
- confronting pent-up anger
- and many other problems.

Introduction

God created marriage and the intellects who invented the high-speed world in which we live. He knew the end from the beginning—on a global scale and in your personal life. He has all the answers you need to succeed in every endeavor, including your marriage. And through the pages of this book, I'll direct you to many of them.

Through chapter after chapter, I will help you identify and resolve what I consider to be the 12 most common causes of stress in marriage. By determining the cause, you can alleviate the harmful stress eating away at your relationship.

I am convinced that the information in this book will empower you to disarm the destructive stress in your life, and increase the intimacy and pleasure you desire in your marriage.

God wants the best for you. He's on your side. He wants to help you eliminate the stress in your life so you can enjoy what you really want—a happy, secure, intimate marriage...for a lifetime.

Jimmy Evans

Chapter One

Defeating Your
Greatest Enemy

Stress is one of the greatest enemies we face in life. And while a certain level of stress is inevitable—and even necessary on a limited and controlled basis—too much stress is devastating to our physical, mental and emotional health.

Unhealthy stress has reached epidemic proportions today. Its effects are felt in every segment of our society. But nowhere are the negative effects of stress felt more than in our marriages.

When we as husbands and wives experience a significant amount of stress, we become emotionally distracted and depleted. We typically become less sensitive to each other's needs. We have less emotional energy. And if the cause of stress and emotional distraction isn't addressed and resolved, then our marriage is usually seriously harmed.

In some cases, the stress in our lives is caused by influences outside our marriages. Basically, our marriage relationship can be healthy, but those outward influences of work, people and events create stress for us or our spouse.

In most cases, however, the real threat to the health of our marriage is caused by internal issues—money, sex, children, in-laws, unresolved anger, and so on. These internal issues create a more serious threat because we tend to place the blame for the stress on each other, rather than on the true source of the problem.

For example, if I'm having a problem with my boss at work, the stress of that problem can affect my wife negatively if I don't handle it properly. But I still have the benefit of seeking refuge in my wife as I come home day after day.

On the other hand, if my wife is the person with whom I am having the conflict, suddenly, I no longer have someone I can "go home to" for refuge and sympathy. The stress becomes compounded and damages our intimacy even more.

> **The signs of stress are all around us. For the most part, however, we tend to deal with stress by trying to deny it, escape from it and sedate it.**

Regardless of where stress comes from, it can—and will—harm our marriages if it isn't resolved in a positive and timely manner.

With that in mind, I have written this book to help you identify and resolve what I consider to be the 12 most common causes of stress in marriage. Without the ability to identify and solve your *real* problems, those problems will produce increasing amounts of stress that will eventually sabotage your marriage.

I am convinced that the information in this book will empower you to disarm the destructive stress in life, stress that would otherwise hinder the intimacy and pleasure you desire in your marriage.

The truth is, God didn't design you to live *under* stress. He created you—and your spouse—to live in paradise. You were meant to live in Eden—a place of pure pleasure and delight. He intended for your lives to be in harmony with Him, with each other and with nature.

God also designed you in such a way that when you stop living according to *His* plan, there are physical and emotional warning signals to help get you out of error and back on track.

Some of the emotional signals of stress include irritability, outbursts of anger, depression, confusion, worry, and an inability to concentrate. Headaches, muscle tension, skin diseases, gastrointestinal and eating disorders, insomnia, and immune deficiency are some of the physical warning signs.

On the spiritual side, all these physical and emotional signs are simply loving messages from God alerting you that you're out of step with His plan. They are His way of telling you that you need to make a change—and now!

The signs of stress are all around us. For the most part, however, we tend to deal with stress by trying to deny it, escape from it and sedate it.

In general, that's why our society is addicted to alcohol, drugs, food, nicotine, sex, gambling, entertainment, and so on. These addictions are attempts to deal with the problems and pressures of life in the most convenient and pleasant way. But they really don't solve anything. In fact, they only add more stress to a person's life, making the cycle even worse.

Yes, things happen in our everyday lives that produce stress. Things happen that are beyond our control.

What *is* in our control, however, is how we confront and deal with those potentially stress-producing events.

Therefore, my challenge to you—*no stress intended*—is to get proactive about the stress you face day in and day out, particularly in your marriage. Identify the sources of stress inside and outside your home.

Then search out the *real* problems behind that stress. Recognize the issues creating the stress in your relationship with your husband or wife—which is what I hope to help you do in this book—and deal with them promptly.

Once you do, you will have uncovered the secret to having a happy, secure, intimate marriage...for a lifetime.

Chapter Two

Resolving the Stress of
The Worst Faulty Spiritual Foundation—Worry

Let's face it, life is bigger than any of us. That's why we need God. And despite the fact we all know worrying won't solve anything...we still do it.

Many people have so perfected worrying that it is a main support in their life's foundation. They consume hours of mental and emotional energy analyzing their problems, going over and over them in their minds. Some even believe that if they didn't "care," they wouldn't worry. They have confused worry with love and trust.

The danger of this obsessive kind of living and thinking is that it is a faulty spiritual foundation, and given the right amount of time, it will utterly destroy you and your marriage. It has ruined many a relationship and torn entire families apart. Simply put, worry isn't of God. It's destructive, and it steals life rather than giving it. Worry is a consuming time bomb.

Jesus warned us all of this. In Matthew 6, Jesus appealed to those listening to Him to stop worrying about the issues of life and start praying. He explained how worrying wouldn't accomplish anything, but trusting in God could accomplish great things.

Two thousand years later, it's still true.

Behind the tension and anxiety of most marriages is *worry*. Worry about money. Worry about work. Worry about the kids, health, and so forth. In fact, worrying has become such a part of life that most people assume it's normal and unavoidable.

Who doesn't worry, right?

Well, believe it or not, there really are many people who don't worry or get stressed out over their problems. And not only are they healthier overall, but they also have much better marriages.

The Inventor of Marriage

To understand the dangers of worry and anxiety and how they can affect your marriage in a negative way, you must first understand that God created man...and marriage. It is not the invention of government or man. When God created marriage, as recorded in Genesis 2, He walked in the Garden of Eden with Adam and Eve. He was their friend and caretaker.

In other words, God created marriage to function with Him as an essential and central part of the relationship. He never intended for a man or a woman to enter into marriage without Him.

Until sin entered the garden and Adam and Eve rebelled against God, they didn't have a care in the world. Life was beautiful as long as they walked with God. Genesis 3, however, records the results of their rejection of God. Shortly after eating the forbidden fruit, Adam rejected Eve, and their relationship was destroyed.

The story of what happened to Adam and Eve is not unique to them. It is a pattern that has been repeated by husbands and wives for thousands of years since.

The Worst Faulty Spiritual Foundation – Worry

The pattern is easy to identify. When a couple depends on the Lord and submits to Him, their lives flourish, both individually and as a couple. But when they rebel against God, or depend on their own resources for success, they soon turn on each other and life becomes bitter.

My wife, Karen, and I experienced this personally many years ago. In fact, it almost cost us our marriage.

When we married more than 28 years ago, I had just received Jesus as my Lord, and so had she. We were new Christians and didn't know much about marriage, much less how to trust God and depend upon Him. What's more, for the first few years of our marriage we never prayed together about anything. I even struggled with praying at all. The Christian life was new to me, and I had a difficult time believing that God really loved me or would answer my prayers.

So, even though Karen expressed a desire for us to pray together on a number of occasions in those first years, I always found an excuse not to do it. My chauvinistic pride kept me from it. After all, I had been raised in a household of "personal responsibility" and "hard work." When things went wrong or difficulties arose, our family did what was necessary to overcome adversity. We *worked* our way to success. We were all successful in the world's terms—and proud of it. It just wasn't like us to admit weakness, or especially to go beyond ourselves for help, which is essentially part of what prayer is.

Consequently, when Karen asked me to pray with her about situations that were bothering her and affecting our marriage, I threw up my guard and insisted that things would be okay and that I could handle it. The problem was, things only grew worse and more out of my control; and eventually, our marriage hit a crisis stage. Even though I claimed to be a born-again Christian, I was a weak spiritual leader in our home. I really did not trust in God.

Furthermore, I had a dominant personality, so I tried to solve my problems with Karen through illegitimate emotional and mental control. Karen chafed under the influence of my overbearing personality, and that was the one issue that nearly cost us our marriage.

As if all that were not enough, rather than admit my weakness and my need for God and Karen, I never let my guard down. My answer to all our problems was to internalize them and worry over them until I came up with a solution. When Karen did not agree with my solution, the fights ensued. And, again, because of my dominant personality, I almost always won. My victories, however, only created more resentment inside of Karen and drove us further apart.

During that time in our marriage, I happened to develop a skin disorder— a rash that appeared in several places on my body. So, I went to the doctor. When the doctor came in to the examining room, he only took a few seconds to look at the rashes. Then he turned and headed out of the room. Before shutting the door, he looked back and said, "The nurse will be in here in just a minute with some information for you."

Information?

I wasn't looking for *information*. I just wanted some medicine so I could get rid of the rash. Several minutes later, a nurse walked into the room and put a cassette tape player on the counter in front of me.

"The doctor wants you to listen to this tape," she said, "and then you can check out."

I was really getting put out with these people. I didn't much care for their kind of "medicine."

As you could probably guess, the tape was all about *worry* and *stress*. It talked about how to deal with stress properly so it wouldn't cause skin diseases...like the one I had.

The Worst Faulty Spiritual Foundation – Worry

Well, the medicine worked. Sitting in the doctor's office that day, I began to realize that my rash was the result of all the worrying I had been doing over the problems Karen and I were going through.

As proud as I had been all of my life that I could solve my own problems, I was now humiliated. In fact, when the cassette finished playing, I had a difficult time walking up to the counter at the doctor's office to check out. I felt like I had been chastised and everyone in the office was looking at me and saying to themselves, "Yeah, there goes that weak, pathetic worrier, Jimmy Evans, with the hideous rashes."

I don't cry very often, but when I got in my car to leave the doctor's office, I was very emotional and I began crying. God met me in my car that day. In His unique way, He used that incident to begin showing me just how much I needed Him...and just how much He loved me.

I wish I could tell you that my life turned around in 24 hours. But it didn't.

In the years that followed, I struggled with the whole idea of God really loving me and wanting to take care of me. I thought I could take care of myself.

Sadly, the real breaking point in my life came when Karen and I almost split up. Our fighting had become more frequent. While I refused to surrender myself completely to the Lord, I kept trying to control Karen and everything else in our home.

Finally, one night we had a horrible fight. I told Karen to pack her bags and get out. As she sobbed in the bedroom, I knew our marriage was on the brink of divorce. That was my breaking point. I got on my knees that night and surrendered control of myself and my marriage to God. When I got up from that prayer, I repented to Karen.

Since that night, more than 23 years ago, our marriage has been different and wonderful. And the one issue that saved our marriage—and continues to be the secret of our success to this day—is our dependence upon God.

A Sure Foundation of Faith

It's important to realize that up until that night, we had a faulty spiritual foundation—one built upon our own strength...upon worry...upon self-reliance.

After that night, we changed from being dependent upon ourselves to being dependent upon God. Since then, individually and as a couple, Karen and I seek God.

We seek Him...

1. In prayer.
2. Through His Word, the Bible.
3. Through Christian relationships in the church.

These three sure foundations of faith have caused our marriage to grow in stability and intimacy, year after year. Each of them is an indispensable element in our maintaining healthy relationships with God and each other.

Without prayer, we worry and trust in ourselves.

Without God's Word, we wander in confusion with no clear direction or lasting solutions.

Without Christian fellowship, we lack the positive support we need to keep us encouraged and accountable.

Of the three sure foundations, prayer is what had the most dramatic effect on the intimacy of our marriage. Even today, it continues to be what changes us the most. As a couple, Karen and I cherish our times of prayer and make them happen, regardless of how busy we are.

In short, we don't worry anymore. We pray.

Having prayed with Karen for years now, I personally am convinced that God loves us and cares for us deeply. I also know He is walking with us in an intimate way, just as He did with Adam and Eve. His presence and power are obvious.

Together, Karen and I have seen thousands of prayers answered in miraculous ways related to our children, our finances, our health, our work, our marriage, and every other issue. When any tensions or worries arise— we pray. And when we pray, peace always comes into our hearts and into our relationship.

Karen and I have also found that, when we put God in control, neither of us is trying to control or manipulate the other. We don't spend all that emotional energy worrying and being stressed out with ourselves or with each other. Instead, we spend our emotional energy loving each other the way God intended.

My friend, worry and stress are curses that are out to destroy your health, happiness and relationships. They are faulty spiritual foundations that God never intended for you to live under. Instead, He intended for you to trust Him to take care of you. That's why Jesus told His followers—as recorded in Matthew 6—not to worry, but to believe that God loved them more than the birds of the air and more than the flowers of the field—both for which He faithfully cares.

Then, Jesus gave this powerful promise: *"Seek first the kingdom of God and His righteousness, and all these things shall be added to you"* (Matthew 6:33).

I can tell you from experience, God keeps this promise.

Build a Stress-Free Foundation

If you will humble yourself before God and before your spouse, and admit your weaknesses and your needs to Him in prayer, He will fulfill His promise to care for you and to give you "all these things."

If you think about it, *all these things* refers to everything you need in life. And most likely, it's everything you worry about. Yes, you can live the rest of your life worrying and caring for yourself. Or, you can pray and trust in God.

But know this: The only way you can ever be successfully married and live in the health and happiness you desire is to build the foundation of your life and marriage upon trust in God.

If you're not quite convinced, realize that *worry* is sin. Simply put, trying to solve your own problems and meet your own needs, rather than trusting in God, is a sin that can devastate your life and marriage.

The story I told about our marriage is common. Having been a marriage counselor for 20 years, it's a story I have heard many times. What I have always seen is that "the" common element in couples who have the best marriages is their relationship with God—both individually and together. They have a daily walk in which they seek God through prayer, through His Word and through Christian fellowship.

On the other hand, I see attractive, sharp, nice couples all of the time who are miserable and cannot solve their problems. They live in an anxiety-filled atmosphere of multiplying problems and mutual finger-pointing.

Though a couple like this may have great potential in their marriage, the stress in their relationship has created an emotional fog that blinds and disorients them. They can no longer see the good in each other that caused them to fall in love. They cannot remember why they married each other in the first place.

The Worst Faulty Spiritual Foundation – Worry

By the time I see a couple like this in the counseling room, it's like they are drowning. They are each thrashing around in troubled waters, trying to get to the surface of their marriage. They are looking for anything to hold on to...because they believe that the end is near.

If that describes you, know that there is something to hold on to, something that can save any troubled or stressed-out marriage. That *something* is God. He is the only lifeline that can truly save any of us. Everything else is a false fix. Nothing else will anchor you or your marriage.

I know. I tried everything before I turned to God. And I ended up with health problems and a marriage that almost sank.

After turning to God, however, my health, my marriage and my happiness have all become secure. What's more, they have flourished.

I'm not saying that when I turned my life over to God, all of my problems—or our problems—went away. What I *am* saying is that when Karen and I began trusting God—and trusting Him together—we were able to turn our problems over to Him, rather than stressing out over them. In turn, God gave us victory over every single problem. Every one of them.

Today, Karen and I still encounter needs, problems and situations that are bigger than we are. But we have learned that God is able to meet those needs.

I don't worry anymore. I pray. I gave up worrying a long time ago, because it was killing me. Worry was killing my marriage and everything around me.

Now, when Karen or I detect the first sign of worry or stress, we turn to God and begin to pray. Not only do we immediately feel more intimate and peaceful, but God also answers our prayers. Today, life with Karen is wonderful. Our life together is full of miracles—thanks to God.

I'm telling you that because your life...with your spouse...can be wonderful, too. If that's what you are after, then you can start by trusting God.

Start by praying together, and do it regularly. Pray about everything. Pray about the issues you both face. Pray about your marriage and your family. I guarantee that you will notice an immediate difference as God's peace descends upon you and you both begin to see the answers to your prayers.

Maybe you're not at a point where you can pray together. Then start by praying individually. Pray for God to work in your marriage.

Perhaps your spouse is not a believer. If that is the case, then the worst thing you could do is to reject your spouse for not being where you are spiritually or try to force "God" on him or her. I suggest you just begin by loving your spouse. Love your husband or wife unconditionally as you hit your knees in prayer. Leave the "fixing" part up to God. Make that your first point of trusting Him to keep His promises on your behalf—and on behalf of your spouse.

Remember, God loves you—He loves your spouse—and He will answer your prayers.

I also encourage you to read Matthew 6 and see for yourself what Jesus says about the love of God for each of us...and how we should trust in Him and not worry.

More than anything, I encourage you to begin today to turn your life over to God and trust Him. God loves you, and He has a great plan for you and your family. But *His* plan can only be accomplished by *His* strength, not yours. And the way you tap into His strength is to acknowledge your weakness, as you trust in His power daily by seeking Him through prayer, through His Word and through His Church.

The Apostle Paul reminds us to *"be anxious for nothing, but in everything by prayer and supplication, with thanksgiving, let your requests be made known to God; and the peace of God, which surpasses all understanding, will guard your hearts and minds through Christ Jesus"* (Philippians 4:6-7).

The Worst Faulty Spiritual Foundation – Worry

Building a strong, sure, spiritual foundation is the most important key to living a life of peace, happiness and marital intimacy.

Chapter Three

Resolving the Stress of
Priority and Time
Conflicts

James and Kyla are a well-educated couple with seemingly everything going for them.

James is an accomplished architect who works for himself and is very successful financially.

Kyla is an ophthalmologist by education. Even though she has a few years of experience, her career is on hold because of her devotion to their 3-year-old twin boys, Nicolas and Jonathan.

I met James and Kyla through a counseling session. Kyla was on the verge of filing for divorce. Her major complaint was that James was never at home and he never had time for her.

Though Kyla would quickly agree that James was a caring and attentive father to the boys, she wasted no time in saying just the opposite about his disposition as a husband. They had been married eight years when I saw them, and Kyla had no intention of making it nine. She wanted out.

My first counseling session with Kyla was without James present, at her request. After about 20 minutes of surface conversation about Kyla, James and their current situation, I asked her why she felt so hopeless about their marriage, and why she felt divorce was the only answer.

Kyla had a hard time putting what she was feeling into words. She began by saying things like, "Well, I really don't love James anymore. I haven't loved him for years, and I guess I'm just now willing to face the truth."

She continued talking about her negative emotions toward James for a couple of minutes.

Then I asked her, "Kyla, what caused you to fall out of love with James?"

With that, Kyla could no longer hide the pain bottled inside her. She spoke a few words, trying to give me an answer, but then lowered her head and began to cry. She stopped trying to put on a facade, and she told me the real reason she was filing for divorce.

"I can't take the pain any longer of being second to James' work," she said.

"I complained for years and did everything I knew to do to attract James to me, but it didn't help. Every time I said something, he just tried to make me feel guilty about putting more pressure on him than he already had. Every time I complained and he rejected me, it just drove us further apart. I don't believe he will ever change, and that is why I want out of the marriage."

Kyla's feelings represent the frustrations of an untold number of wives. Even though the problem isn't "another woman," these wives' feelings are basically the same as if their husbands were cheating on them. They feel this way because God created marriage to be the highest priority in our lives, with the exception of our personal relationship with God.

In Genesis 2:24, just after God created Adam, Eve, and the marriage covenant, He stated that, for the sake of marriage, a man would have to "leave" his father and mother in order to be joined to his wife. We know when God said this that He wasn't just speaking to Adam and Eve, because they didn't have a mother. God had personally created them.

God was, in fact, telling Adam and Eve—and all of us—that marriage would require the highest level of priority to operate successfully. He was saying that marriage was even more important than our closest blood kin, our parents.

If you don't honor marriage as the highest priority in your life, your marriage will not work. Your spouse will become jealous of what has taken his or her place in your life.

> **If you don't honor marriage as the highest priority in your life, it doesn't work, and your spouse will become jealous of what has taken his or her place in your life.**

That was the issue facing Kyla. While she didn't understand the deeper spiritual truths I just explained, she did know that she was deeply jealous of James' career.

Kyla had fallen in love with James when they were both in undergraduate studies at the same university. She remembered the times when it seemed that all they had was each other. Those were the "good times." Nothing came before their time together every day. Even the demanding studies and part-time employment during their college years didn't detract from their mutual devotion.

The Law of Priority

After marriage, however, everything changed for James and Kyla. Their relationship went sour, and it was all because they had both violated the first law of marriage—the law of priority.

When I say that they *both* violated the law of priority, I mean that there is another side to the story.

A week after speaking with Kyla, James agreed to meet with me. He was sharply dressed, articulate and very honest. In fact, it didn't take him long to get down to business after we started our session.

James started out by saying, "I know Kyla told you about the problems we are having, and that I work too much."

I nodded my head in affirmation.

"Well, I do work too much," he went on to say, "and I know I have to stop. I have gone through some difficult times with employees for the past several years. Just when I think I have the right person hired, they quit or start their own business and I'm left picking up the pieces. It has put a lot of pressure on me and on our marriage, but I think I have my business in order now and can focus more on Kyla and the boys."

After James finished, I started probing around his feelings toward Kyla to see if there were any deeper issues, beyond employee problems or work stress, that were causing him to avoid her by going to work. I did that because, over years of counseling couples, I have found that a person's outward behavior is rarely the root issue of the problem. Typically, what people are doing on the outside reveals inward issues they are either denying or just simply refusing to deal with in a direct manner.

As I questioned James, he gave me the typical "Everything is OK" line.

Then I asked, "James, when you look back in the past in your marriage, are there any unresolved hurts or offenses you have toward Kyla?"

James looked toward the ceiling and said, "No, not that I can think of."

"Have there been any problems over sex, money, the kids, or anything like that you haven't resolved with her?" I continued.

"No, not that I can remember," he replied. "Sure, we've had disagreements, but I think we've gotten through them OK."

Then I hit a nerve.

"How about issues like your in-laws or your parents or friends or things like that? Have you ever dealt with those kinds of things?"

At first, James looked as though he were going to deny problems in those areas, too. But then he got silent and looked down. He started breathing deeply like he was frustrated or trying to make a decision of whether or not to open up to me.

Finally, he did.

As it turned out, James had a lot of debt because of college loans. Kyla didn't have any because her parents paid for all her education. Even when they got married, Kyla's parents paid for all her graduate studies.

It was Kyla who worried about their finances. With a faulty foundation of worry, Kyla made some wrong decisions – decisions that now were destroying her marriage.

When James first got out of school and started working for an architectural firm, he wasn't making very much money, and Kyla had just gotten pregnant with the boys. At that point, James worked out on paper how he and Kyla could make it financially, even though she would have to quit working when she had the twins.

Still, it was Kyla who worried about their finances. With a faulty foundation of worry, Kyla made some wrong decisions—decisions that now were destroying her marriage.

James got to the root of his feelings: "Kyla would bring up the issue of my college loans in a way that always made me feel guilty. It made me angry and it became a sticking point in our relationship.

"What violated me the most, however, was when she borrowed the money from her parents to pay off my loans without asking me...."

One day, James came home after work only to find his in-laws there, waiting to tell him how they had paid off his student loans and that he could pay them back whenever he could. His father-in-law then went into a long speech about money management and how James needed to learn to handle money.

"I tried to remain calm and contain myself," James confessed, "even though I felt totally violated by everything that was happening.

"As soon as Kyla's parents left, I blew up. That was several years ago, and she has never agreed that she was wrong for getting her parents' help without asking me. In fact, when I bring it up, she tries to make me feel guilty because I'm not more appreciative of what her parents have done.... Maybe that's why I find excuses to work so much."

It didn't take long to see that James and Kyla had drawn a "battle line" and neither of them was willing to acknowledge their errors. James' battle line was over Kyla's parents and the secret money transaction. Kyla's was James' distraction from her and his chronic overworking.

The truth was, both were violated by something that had taken their place as the high priority they once were. Worse still, both had a justification for their behavior that failed to calm each other's jealousy.

How to Make Your Spouse— And Your Marriage—Your Priority

In marriage counseling, this kind of scenario is actually common. It's a situation that places a lot of stress on the relationship.

In James and Kyla's case, they were willing to receive what I told them about the vicious cycle of their problems. They both acknowledged their mistakes and changed.

Kyla admitted to James that she was wrong to call her parents without his knowledge and agreement. James admitted to Kyla that he had been using his work as an excuse to stay away from her and to punish her. He had been willing to make the sacrifices necessary to be with his children, but not the ones necessary to be with his wife. It was a happy ending to a story that many times ends unhappily.

While you may or may not be able to relate to the specific problems James and Kyla faced, I'm certain you do face challenges in managing your time and your priorities in life. To help you resolve these conflicts successfully and keep your marriage on the higher level of priority where it belongs, I want to suggest three steps you can take that *will* make a difference:

1.   *Give your marriage first priority in "real" terms, not just words.*

Many people say the right words to their spouses about their love and devotion, but they never demonstrate that love and devotion in *real* terms. Therefore, the violated spouse is seldom comforted by empty words and promises.

Marriage was created by God to be the first priority in your life, with the exception of your relationship with Him. And while you may *verbally* insist that you love your spouse, here are four ways priorities are proven in what I call "real" terms:

Sacrifice—If your spouse is a priority to you, then you should be willing to sacrifice things of lower priority for him or her. If your spouse is not a priority, then *he or she* will be the one sacrificed for your real priorities.

At the same time, being unwilling to sacrifice is the root issue of why so many people live under enormous stress and constant and unyielding time demands.

Remember the priority God gave marriage in Genesis 2?

When He said we would have to be willing to leave our parents for the sake of our marriage, He wasn't telling us that forsaking our parents would always be required. He was telling us that if there was a priority conflict between our parents and our marriage, then we would have to be willing to sacrifice our relationship with our parents to protect our marriage.

Parents, work, children, school activities, friends, church, soccer—all of these are competing for attention.

But without a clear, set list of priorities — and the willingness to sacrifice things of a lower priority to protect the higher ones – you will live under constant stress as the lesser priorities rob you of the most precious things in life.

But without a clear, set list of priorities—and the willingness to sacrifice things of a lower priority to protect the higher ones—you will live under constant stress as the lesser priorities rob you of the most precious things in life.

To conquer the stress that comes from constant conflicts among priorities, you simply must come to the point of realizing you cannot "have it all." The penalty of trying to *have it all* is losing your health, happiness and relationships with God and your family.

Therefore, accept the fact that you cannot have everything or do everything in life, and decide right now that you are going to sacrifice the *less* important things in life to keep the *most* important things healthy.

Time—*Time* is the commodity of relationship and it must be distributed according to priority.

For example, if God is truly *first place* in your life, then you will honor the Sabbath Day without complaint. But if you are only giving lip service to God and something else really has His place in your life, then you will not observe the Sabbath to pursue Him, and you will chafe at the obligation.

The same applies to your spouse.

If your husband or wife is truly a priority, then you will give him or her a dedicated and protected amount of your time. If you do not hold your spouse at that higher level of priority, then you will complain when he or she requires—or demands—your time. I believe that this is the most telling sign when the priority of a marriage has failed. And the results are very evident...you "fall in love" when you spend time with your spouse. You "fall out of love" when you don't.

Attitude—When a man and woman first meet, they not only prioritize each other, but they also demonstrate an attitude of *pleasure* about it.

Oftentimes, however, after a man and woman marry, they may not have priorities that are more important than each other, and they may even spend a great deal of time together, but they do it with the wrong attitude. They start acting as though pursuing each other and meeting one another's needs is a "ball and chain" that they are sentenced to drag with them through life. Their attitude translates as rejection for their spouse.

You may not realize it, but you communicate to everyone around you what your real priorities in life are by an attitude of desire and delight. Rejection and lower priorities are revealed through your attitude of apathy and obligation—*Do I really have to do this?...Well, OK.*

Energy—Priorities must include *all* the assets of life to be genuine. If you are telling your spouse, "Oh, Sweetheart, you know you are number one in my life..." but you are withholding the energy that it takes to keep your husband or wife in that place, then you are lying. You are holding back in order to give to something or someone else.

Again, people fall in love because they do whatever it takes to give their relationship the time and energy it needs. They sacrifice. They pour into their relationship at the expense of everything else.

The reason people fall out of love is because they get lazy. They stop working at the relationship and then wonder why it doesn't work.

Your energy—your supply—is essential in making your relationship with your spouse successful, and keeping it *first place* in real terms.

2. *Protect your marriage from "lower" priorities.*

Most of the things that ruin a marriage are not "bad" things. They are simply *good things* that are out of priority. Work, children, family, friends, hobbies—none of these are bad. Yet, any of them can destroy a marriage.

Take children as an example. They are a blessing from God, but they are not as important as your marriage—which is a surprise to many parents. Certainly, you must highly prioritize your children. You must love and care for them. But your parenting will only be for 18 or so years. Your marriage, on the other hand, will last a lifetime.

When Karen and I first married, there were no children in our home competing for our time and attention. Today, we do not have children in our home, because our kids are grown and married. While we have a wonderful relationship with them, they want to live their own lives. They don't want us intruding.

My point is, Karen and I are grateful we made the sacrifices necessary to raise good children. But we are also grateful that we didn't sacrifice our marriage for them by letting them come before us. In doing so, our children saw us "in love" and they grew up in a home with a stable marriage that provided a solid foundation and example for them.

The problem with sacrificing your marriage for the sake of your children is that it is shortsighted and sets you and your children up for dysfunctional relationships.

Look at it this way: If you earned a million dollars a year and received great honor in doing so, but went home at the end of each day to a terrible marriage—what good would all that money be? We all know that when our marriage is rotten, it doesn't really matter what else is good in life, because we are still miserable.

So, regardless of what delights or demands come into your life, one of the disciplines of a successful marriage is to protect the priority of your marriage against the "bad" *and* "good" things that seek to violate the position of your spouse in your life.

3. *Budget time the same as you would money.*

Violated priorities and stressed-out lives are almost always accompanied by a host of lame excuses and empty promises. Yes, our intentions may be good, but they never seem to translate into reality.

Why?

Oftentimes, it's because we are poor *time* managers.

For example, I have a friend who was always late to everything. As a result, he was forever "in trouble" with his wife, his kids, his employer, his employees, and so on.

Now, I've never met a man who was a better person at heart, yet a more miserable liar when it came to appointments or being faithful to what he said.

One day, my friend was very late for an appointment with me. When he showed up, he gave me the same old excuse, "I'm sorry—I just didn't realize my last appointment would take so long."

Though I was frustrated with him, I realized he was caught in a trap and didn't know how to get out. So, I taught him something that day—which, according to him, revolutionized his life.

I told my friend that if time were money, he would be bankrupt.

The greater priorities in life are owed first and must be paid regularly. Ruined marriages are often the result of very sincere people who became bankrupt in their relationship because they didn't budget their time prudently. The stresses and demands of life dictated their behavior.

With a background in business, he understood the analogy. I explained how time is a limited commodity, just like money. But, unlike money, we all have the same amount of time. And if we want to end up in the "profit" margin, then we must balance our assets against our expenses.

Then I told my friend how everyone around him was frustrated with him and why. I helped him see how he was constantly borrowing time from God, his wife, his children, his friends, and others, to pay people time that he didn't need to be paying them.

The bottom line was, he was deep in debt to the "important" people in his life because he continued to allow the "less" important people to rob him of his assets—time. It was as though he were out buying an expensive suit of clothes with the money he should have been using to pay his last month's electric bill. It will eventually lead to big problems.

The greater priorities in life are owed *first* and must be paid *regularly*. Ruined marriages are often the result of very sincere people who became bankrupt in their relationship because they didn't budget their time prudently. The stresses and demands of life dictated their behavior.

Rather than being proactive and deciding in advance what they would and would not do, they reacted and became victims of a stressed-out, undisciplined lifestyle.

To keep your marriage and life healthy and free from harmful stress, budget your time as you would your money. You can do that by sitting down and listing on a piece of paper the most important people and things in your life.

Your list might look something like this:

- God
- My spouse
- My children
- Me
- Church
- Work
- My friends

After making your list, take out a calendar and—beginning with your most important priorities—schedule regular, dedicated time for them.

The further down the list you get, the more you will likely see that it doesn't take long before you run out of time. That's usually when it dawns on you that you've been robbing time from the most important people in your life...only to give it to less important things on your list.

Just as with financial budgeting, you have to make difficult choices sometimes in order to be successful. And, yes, that means some of your desires will go undeveloped. Some friendships will go unattended. Some interests will go unpursued. Some demands will go unmet. Still, the most important people on your list *must* be paid regularly with the time that is due them. That is the only way you can ensure lasting success and happiness in marriage, and in life.

What's more, you must also teach your children to budget their time properly and to make the necessary sacrifices. As never before, families are being stressed out by the constant demands, desires and opportunities of their children. Again, while we as parents have the responsibility to sacrifice when necessary to meet our children's needs and accommodate their interests, the reality is that we live in a "driven" culture. Parents often escort their children from school...to sports...to music lessons...to entertainment...to the friend's house...to shopping....

It's a never-ending cycle of packed schedules—and the stress that comes with it.

The stress doesn't just affect the children, however. It affects the entire family, especially mom and dad's marriage.

Before long, the joy of life is robbed, and family relationships begin to fall apart because there is no quality time or energy left for each other. The dreams of peaceful, intimate family times are robbed by a lack of time management combined with the desire to "have it all"—and for our children to "have it all."

You and your spouse must work together to establish the standards and traditions that will keep your priorities protected and your relationship healthy. You must also set a good example for your children by managing your schedules properly, so you have quality time and energy for each other, as well as your children.

But don't stop there. Train your children to do the same. You want them to be blessed with a full and fun life, but you must understand that their relationship with God and family is the essential foundation for their true happiness and success, just as it is with yours.

No matter how good your children may be at gymnastics or soccer, or how popular they are among their friends, their happiness is mostly dependent upon the quality of their home life.

The sad truth is, society is unraveling before us. While our children have never had so much and have never been able to do so much, neither have they had greater opportunity to be so empty and so confused.

Parents, realize that behind that emptiness and confusion is the lack of moral and practical guidance from us—their moms and dads.

Don't allow your children to become so busy because it keeps them "out of your hair" for a while. That's a wrong motive. Computers, movies, television, friends, activities—nothing can take your place.

To sum it all up—do whatever it takes to create a lifestyle that allows you to love and prioritize your spouse and your children in real terms...and on a regular basis. Your home is where you will find the real joy in life. Nothing else can take the place of *home* in your heart.

Your marriage is the most important relationship you will ever have on this earth. God made it that way. But for it to be the success you—and He—want it to be, you must make it a high priority. You must dedicate and protect the resources necessary for a successful marriage. Only then can you calm the stress and relieve the pressure that is out to destroy it.

Chapter Four

Resolving the Stress of
Unresolved Anger and Chronic Conflicts

Now that we have laid something of a foundation concerning stress and marriage, I want to address an issue that has a huge impact on the intimacy of your marriage. This issue will determine whether or not you will live with chronic stress...or genuine peace.

The issue is dealing with anger and resolving conflicts.

No matter how good your marriage may be, anger and conflict are inevitable in any relationship. For that reason, you need to learn skills to deal with them properly. If you know how to deal with anger, then you have ensured that your marriage will remain intimate and healthy.

On the other hand, if you never learn how to go head-to-head with anger and conflict and overcome them, then you have ensured that negative feelings will accumulate until a blanket of bitterness and discouragement smothers the passion in your marriage.

Marriage expert Gary Smalley describes anger as a "toxic waste" that is the most destructive force in marriage. I agree.

Unresolved anger can cause a couple to go from passionate love on their wedding day to bitter hate on the day of their divorce. As real and intense as their love was early in their relationship, the divorcing couple has long lost those feelings. Instead, the accumulation of anger in their souls has created such intense negativity and stress that they are willing to abandon the relationship to avoid more pain.

> **If you never learn how to go head-to-head with anger and conflict and overcome them, then you have ensured that negative feelings will accumulate until a blanket of bitterness and discouragement smothers the passion in your marriage.**

Even if a couple doesn't divorce, unrehe intimacy of their marriage. It keeps them from being able to speak openly the way they once did. It also inhibits their sexual intimacy as it turns down the emotional thermostat of their relationship. Eventually, their unresolved anger wilsolved anger kills tl cause them to avoid emotional intimacy for fear that the unresolved issue or issues will surface.

So, even if a couple with chronic problems decides to stick it out and stay together, their unresolved anger will gradually cause their relationship to decay.

It's Never Too Late to Do What's Right

When anger is addressed properly and removed from a marriage, the husband's and wife's emotions will remain healthy and can even be resurrected.

I've counseled many couples who have had years of unresolved issues between them. They usually come to see me because they have finally grown so miserable that they decide to "try" counseling. Most of them openly admit they have been out of love for a long time. But I've had the joy of watching many of them fall passionately in love again after resolving their long-standing conflicts.

I've learned that it is never too late to do what is right.

If you are a couple who wants to avoid serious problems and remain healthy from the start, you must learn the skills for dealing with anger properly. That's why for the remainder of this chapter I want to give you three biblical truths that will help you press through anger and conflict every time. They come from Ephesians 4:26-27:

"Be angry, and do not sin: do not let the sun go down on your wrath, nor give place to the devil."

Here, the Apostle Paul is writing to the church at Ephesus. He is telling them how to have the kind of loving relationships that honor God and keep bitterness and anger from destroying His purposes for their lives. Paul recognized the threat of unresolved anger, so he gave three simple instructions concerning it.

1. *Admit your anger.*

Notice how Paul starts verse 26 with "Be angry...."

Some people readily admit and demonstrate their anger, while others bottle it up inside themselves. When Karen and I married, I expressed my anger openly, but I was unrighteous and intimidating in how I did it.

Karen, on the other hand, was constantly feeling angry and violated because of my behavior, but she bottled up her anger on the inside.

Both extremes are unhealthy and dangerous, yet the more dangerous tendency is to bottle up the anger and not be honest about it. I would add that this is true with the exception of people who express their anger in ways that are significantly volatile.

Bottled-up anger is dangerous because it will eventually implode and explode.

Imploding anger damages the person who is storing it, because we were designed by God to be temples for His Spirit, not repositories for toxic emotions. There is simply no place within us that anger can be stored safely, so that's why we must admit it and let it come into the light.

One of the most common but unknown results of bottling up unresolved anger is depression. Interestingly, one of the clinical definitions of depression is "anger turned inward."

Anger is a very high emotional consumer. When unresolved, it puts our emotions on a treadmill that never cuts off. Whether it takes an hour, a day or a month, the time will come when our emotions will collapse—just like a runner would who never quit running. When those emotions collapse, it is because of the consuming force of anger within.

Unresolved anger is one reason why depression has become an epidemic in our society. We simply cannot ignore or try to sedate unhealthy feelings and hope to be truly happy.

The danger, especially among Christians, is that many are ashamed of their emotions. They equate their anger as a sign of being "unspiritual" or wrong.

Granted, anger can be a sign of immaturity, unrealistic expectations, misunderstandings, and the like, yet we need to understand two important aspects about anger.

One—God gets angry.

If anger were always wrong, then surely God would not do it. But in His case, He always gets angry for the right reasons.

Certainly, there are times when we get angry because something inside is wrong, something that needs to be changed. Other times, however, we get angry because we have genuinely been violated.

Read the story of Jesus cleansing the temple. He was angry—and rightly so. And He made no bones about it.

The point is, you can be angry and righteous at the same time.

Two—even though your reason for being angry may not be "right," that doesn't mean you just try to cover the anger or ignore it. Many people incorrectly assume that if they could possibly be wrong in their anger, then they should not talk about it.

Of course, there are times when we might have a slight sense of anger rise up within us, but only to a degree that is of no consequence. In that case, we may sit on it for a day or two and find that it goes away without a negative impact on our marriage, or on our ability to give and receive love.

Then there are those times when anger seems to flash through our entire being, and while we may or may not be right in how we feel, the anger does not go away. It keeps us from relating to our spouse properly. We must not allow the anger to linger in the shadows. We simply must be honest about our feelings, letting our spouse know that we realize that we could be wrong, but we just need to talk about it. Admitting anger and getting it into the light is an essential practice for healthy emotions and marriages.

Maybe you're thinking your marriage is too far gone and you couldn't possibly be honest with your spouse about your feelings. If that is true, start by being honest with God. Open your heart to Him, which in turn will allow His light to shine into your hurts and frustrations, and bring healing and peace.

Then, consider going for help. If your marriage is in serious condition, having a third person acting as a mediator can help you and your spouse to hear each other. Having another person can also help navigate you both through your negative emotions, which is very helpful, if not essential. Find a good Christian leader or counselor, and ask your spouse to go with you.

Another important aspect of admitting your anger in marriage is having the understanding with your spouse that you both have the right to complain. Being allowed to complain about something that bothers you is vital to a healthy marriage.

In unhealthy marriages, there is often an attitude demonstrated by one or both spouses that they do not want to hear the complaints of the other person. This attitude is normally accompanied by behavior that punishes the complaining spouse.

I have heard many sad stories over the years, and typically, it is the wife who comes to me looking for counsel. After telling me all her complaints about her husband, I will almost always ask, "Have you told your husband this?"

And, usually, she will say something like, "My husband would go ballistic if I told him what I just told you. He hates it when I tell him something is wrong."

A few years ago, I had a similar encounter with a frustrated husband. He and his wife were having big problems. Though the husband admitted that he was as much of the problem as his wife was, he was frustrated by the fact that he couldn't say anything negative to his wife without her going into an emotional fit that would last for days. She would scream and cry when he complained. Then she would withdraw from him emotionally and physically until he would finally admit that he was wrong.

This had been going on for more than 20 years, and the husband was ready to divorce. In his mind, he only had two choices: He could let his wife control the relationship by letting her have her way and never complain again. Or, he could stand his ground and pay the price of her fits and withdrawal. Obviously, both scenarios were depressing for him.

The solution was that she had to learn to let him tell her things that were wrong. She had to give him the freedom to complain!

Going back to Ephesians 4 and the truth that we should deal with our anger by admitting it, Paul was telling the people to be honest about their emotions, regardless of how wrong or negative their feelings may have been.

With that truth in mind, it is important to understand that two telling features of dysfunctional families are *silence* and *shame*. If something is wrong in a dysfunctional family, there is a "code of silence" that is not to be broken. If someone breaks that code, then that person is shamed by the others.

"How could you say something like that?"

"If you don't have anything positive to say, then just keep your mouth shut."

"Don't you see the damage you are causing?"

Those are typical comments used to shame and silence the one who is trying to express honest feelings.

Problems don't go away just because we choose not to hear about them. That's like throwing trash downstairs in the basement, then shutting the door and believing it's gone. Not only is it still there, but the growing stench will be a constant reminder of its presence.

That's exactly how I treated Karen when we were first married. I expressed my complaints to Karen, but I did not want to hear them from her. And when she did complain, I shamed her and rejected her.

One of Karen's running complaints was the amount of time I spent playing golf with my friends...away from her and the kids. I made her so miserable every time she brought it up that she finally stopped talking about it.

The problem didn't go away. It was just operating underground. It was churning deep within her heart, doing even more damage.

That issue almost destroyed our relationship. I wouldn't let Karen complain and be honest about her feelings.

We must give our spouses the right to complain and express honest feelings if we are going to keep destructive anger out of our relationships and be able to resolve our problems. If we do not give them that right, then we are being selfish and showing an unwillingness to accept their influence in the marriage. We're basically telling them that we don't care about their feelings and we're not willing to take responsibility to work at the relationship.

Problems don't go away just because we choose not to hear about them. That's like throwing trash downstairs in the basement, then shutting the door and believing it's gone. Not only is it still there, but the growing stench will be a constant reminder of its presence.

The same is true in marriage. The decreasing intimacy and growing tension in the relationship will be a constant reminder that anger hasn't left, but instead, it is piling up down in the basement.

Some of the best research on the subject of conflict in marriage has been conducted by Dr. John Gottman at the University of Washington. Through many years of study on the subject, Dr. Gottman can predict within 93 percent accuracy a couple's chance of divorce.

He does this by using four common traits he has noticed in failing marriages over the years. The degree that these four elements are present in a relationship is the degree of likelihood for divorce. These four issues are so foreboding to the hopes of a good marriage that Dr. Gottman calls them the "Four Horsemen of the Apocalypse."

Dr. Gottman's four predictors of divorce are:

Criticism—the tone of negativity in the relationship. This is not "healthy" complaining. It's unhealthy sarcasm. It's a spirit of criticism. This is in contrast to the praise, love-talk and positive spirit of a good relationship.

Defensiveness—not allowing a spouse to complain or have an influence in making decisions. It rejects a spouse's input as invalid. It indirectly accuses them of being the problem.

Contempt—as wine is grape juice that has fermented over time, contempt is fermented anger. More than criticism, contempt is a deeply abiding anger that has forgotten the good in the other person as it sees and speaks the worst about them.

Stonewalling—refusing to deal with an issue. Stonewalling is always present in a divorce situation. One or both spouses withdraw from discussing a problem and refuse to change.

Seeing any one of these four issues in your marriage does not mean your marriage is doomed and can never work. It is simply a sign that your marriage needs help. Heeding warning signs and making the right decisions to change things can save any marriage, no matter how far gone it may seem.

Most importantly, remember that no problem is too great for God to fix. But He does require honesty from you if He's going to work for your good. In marriage, there are two parts to honesty—the willingness to be honest, and the willingness to receive honesty.

If you are willing to be honest and cultivate an atmosphere of openness in your life and marriage, you will succeed—because God works in the light. If you are not willing to be honest, however, you will fail—because Satan works in the dark.

You can start by telling your spouse that you are committed to meeting his or her needs, and to working to make your marriage successful. Tell your husband or your wife that, if there are any complaints, you want to know what they are and that you are ready to listen...respectfully.

That simple step will lay a solid foundation of trust and openness in your marriage. It will pay you dividends for a lifetime.

2. *Submit your emotions.*

In Ephesians 4:26-27, Paul's second instruction concerning the threat of unresolved anger can be summed up as *submit it.*

First, Paul said, "Be angry...," but now he puts a parameter on your honesty.

Submit your emotions to the Lord and walk in obedience to what you know is His will.

I have counseled many couples who responded to anger with threats of divorce or affairs, horrible cursing and name-calling, physical and emotional abuse, and so on. Though common, these are illegitimate expressions of anger.

When you are angry, be honest about it. And then turn that anger over to God. Ask Him to help you find the truth in your feelings. Don't let your feelings dictate to you what is "true."

Pray something like this:

"Lord, I'm feeling angry and I submit my emotions to you. If they are valid,

please help me express them in the right way. If they are invalid, help me express them in the right way and be able to receive the truth about them from You, my spouse, or others around me."

Once you've done that, allow the Holy Spirit to fill you—which is especially true when dealing with negative emotions.

Galatians 5 gives us only two choices related to how we are going to live. We are either going to live by the power of our flesh, or, we're going to live by the power of God's Spirit.

In this passage, Paul contrasts the deeds of the flesh with the fruits of the Holy Spirit. The deeds of the flesh include outbursts of anger, division, enmity and jealousy. The fruits of the Spirit are love, joy, peace, patience, kindness, goodness, faithfulness, gentleness and self-control.

Each of us is very limited in the ability to respond to negative emotions. We have a very limited amount of emotional strength that is exhausted quickly. Without the help of the Holy Spirit, our emotions are like a car engine without oil. They overheat and lock down quickly.

With the Holy Spirit flowing through us, however, our emotions are empowered and protected. What would have caused us to blow a gasket yesterday, we can calmly get through today, if we will allow the Holy Spirit to fill us.

Couples must have the abiding presence of the Holy Spirit in their lives to be successfully married. Every fruit of the Spirit is a relational quality. It is nothing less than the personality of God being transmitted through us as we yield to Him and trust Him in the challenges of life.

In dealing with anger, never justify your sin.

"You made me so mad, I couldn't help myself!"

That kind of excuse is self-deception.

Regardless of how angry you get, you can *always* choose to do the right thing.

As I once heard, "Life doesn't form you. Your response to life forms you."

Using other people's behavior as an excuse to justify your sin is weak. You must choose to do the right thing, in spite of what others do. In doing so, your behavior will fix the problem behind the anger as it gains the blessing and partnership of God. Anything else will only keep the vicious cycles of life turning against you.

3. *Deal with today's anger—today. Forgive.*

Paul's third and final instruction concerning anger is not to let the sun go down on it. If you do, you will give the devil opportunity in your life.

One of the most critical disciplines of a good marriage is not to go to bed with unresolved anger. Going to bed angry does several things that are devastating to a marriage.

First, it develops a habit pattern of allowing problems to exist without being confronted openly and in a timely manner.

Second, going to bed angry kills the passion of your relationship. Remember, anger is like toxic waste. It was never meant to be stored inside you—and when it is, it is always destructive. It destroys your outlook on life and love.

Think about it. Yesterday, without anger, you were able to look at a flower bed and see beautiful colors and smell wonderful fragrances. Today—being enraged with anger—you pass by the same flower bed and see bugs and smell fertilizer. What a difference a day of anger makes in a relationship!

The most devastating problem that unresolved anger brings is an open door for the devil. The Apostle Paul makes this point trying to compel us to deal with anger in a timely manner.

Why is the devil such a threat when it comes to unresolved anger? To begin with, Satan is an accuser and slanderer by nature. Unresolved anger gives him an open door to accuse a spouse of his or her motives.

I have counseled many men and women who truly felt as though they were married to the devil himself. Even though they once had deep feelings for their spouses, they became convinced their spouses were evil.

How did that happen?

They innocently went to bed with anger, thereby opening wide the door to the accuser.

Marriage was created by God to be the most sacred of all human institutions. For that reason, Satan loves divorce because it damages the people God loves and prevents God's sacred plan from coming to pass. Anger is ultimately the devil's method to divide couples and destroy lives.

Remember, there's no problem with *today's* anger. Today's anger is manageable. It's *yesterday's* anger that is the problem. Yesterday's anger has had time to ferment and turn into contempt. Yesterday's anger has visited overnight with the accuser of your spouse.

Remember, there's no problem with today's anger. Today's anger is manageable. It's yesterday's anger that is the problem. Yesterday's anger has had time to ferment and turn into contempt. Yesterday's anger has visited overnight with the accuser of your spouse.

So, if you want to remove anger from your marriage once and for all, you must deal with it in a timely manner—every time. Then, of course, you must be willing to forgive.

Forgiveness in the biblical sense means to "forgive a debt."

True forgiveness means I forgive whatever debt you owed me for your wrongdoing, and I will not make you pay later or bring it up in the future. It is forgiven.

When a spirit of forgiveness is present in a marriage, love blossoms and grows. When a spouse or a couple holds grudges, brings up the past, and generally won't forgive, it ruins the intimacy of a relationship.

Jesus said if we didn't forgive others, He would not forgive us (Matthew 6:18). We need grace, so therefore, we must be willing to give it.

This issue of forgiveness also applies to people in your past—parents, siblings, friends, ex-spouses, business partners. It applies to anyone who may have wronged you. Even if your bitterness isn't toward your spouse, he or she is still directly affected by it.

> **Removing anger always means that you either forgive others, or you receive forgiveness from others, including God. It even means forgiving yourself. But no matter what direction the forgiveness is flowing, it must flow for love to remain healthy.**

In fact, families normally take the brunt of every negative emotion you feel, even if they didn't cause it. That's why forgiving others is so important. It clears your heart of polluted feelings, thereby allowing you to give—and receive—in a pure manner.

Removing anger always means that you either forgive others, or you receive forgiveness from others, including God. It even means forgiving yourself. But no matter what direction the forgiveness is flowing, it must *flow* for love to remain healthy.

Unresolved Anger and Chronic Conflicts

For your marriage to be successful, you must learn to deal with anger in a timely manner and to resolve conflicts properly. If an issue is so difficult that you and your spouse cannot resolve it between yourselves, then it is vitally important that you go outside of the marriage for help.

Getting help is not a sign of weakness. It is a sign of wisdom. The best marriages I see are not between two people who are always able to resolve their problems. The best marriages I see are between two people who are committed to working through their problems and are willing to be taught by others.

There is one final point I need to make about resolving anger and conflicts in marriage. As we are honest about our feelings and are committed to dealing with our anger day in and day out, it is important that we learn how to communicate our feelings to our spouses without making them feel threatened. When you feel angry, or you have some other negative emotion that you need to discuss, you need to begin your confrontation with words of love and affirmation.

"We're on the same team, and I'm committed to our marriage...."

One couple I know uses those words every time they confront each other. Likewise, you must never begin with a harsh countenance or hostile words.

The research of Dr. John Gottman revealed that a harsh "start up" to a conversation dooms it to failure. He discovered that a conversation never rises above the tone of the first three minutes. It is important, then, that you begin every conversation in a positive and respectful manner.

Also, while communicating feelings, it is important that you share how you are feeling without trying to enforce your feelings on your spouse. In other words, you can tell your spouse how you feel about something. But it's wrong to try to tell your spouse what he or she meant by what was said.

Proper complaining in marriage always points the finger at yourself and how you feel. That allows you to express yourself without making your spouse feel threatened or attacked.

This "I feel" approach is almost always successful because it puts the spotlight on you while admitting that your feelings could be wrong. It leaves the door open for your spouse to bring his or her perspective into play without having been painted into a corner.

Finally, after you have expressed yourself to your spouse, it's important that he or she have an opportunity to speak without being attacked.

Listen carefully to what your spouse has to say. Do not interrupt. And when he or she is finished speaking, affirm what was said. Doing so will affirm your spouse's feelings as valid—even if you don't agree with those feelings.

Dealing with your negative feelings—confronting anger—in a timely and respectful manner develops an atmosphere of trust. Trust is a crucial element that allows you to resolve anger as you grow in intimacy with your spouse.

Don't allow *destructive* anger to remain in your marriage. Begin today by admitting your anger and allowing the Lord to give you the wisdom and power to deal with it properly. As you do, you will invest in a marriage that will produce a lifetime of rewards.

Chapter Five

Resolving the Stress of
Money Problems and
Financial Disagreements

Of all the enemies that can attack the intimacy and security of a marriage, money problems are among the most serious and destructive. In fact, they are the number one reason why couples divorce.

But while the stress of money can be a marriage killer, there is another side to it.

One of the greatest potential blessings of the marriage relationship is the benefit that it can provide financially. Statistically, married couples are better off financially than single or divorced people. The reason for this is twofold.

First of all, being married allows couples to live more economically than when they are single. They are able to combine resources and save on many expenses such as housing and utilities.

Second, being married provides a stability in their lives that causes them to make better long-term financial decisions.

Without a doubt, marriage provides the basis for greater financial blessings. The key, however, is to find a way to achieve financial dreams without being hindered by the common problems that sabotage so many couples.

In counseling couples over the years, as well as in my own marriage, I have seen four common problems that produce damaging financial stress. By introducing you to these root issues and helping you understand them, you can easily avoid or solve them in your marriage.

Respecting Your Spouse's Perspective and Input

In the first ten years of our marriage, some of the most serious arguments Karen and I had were about money. As we fought, we often rejected each other's input.

Karen resented it when I spent any significant amount of money and often accused me of being impulsive. I resented Karen's comments and often accused her of being controlling and tight. Around and around we would go over the "money issues" until one day we finally realized what it was doing to our marriage, and we learned how to stop it.

Our first great revelation that helped us to stop judging and rejecting each other was that our differences about money were normal and even helpful. The truth is, most husbands and wives view money differently.

One of the most intriguing studies I've ever read on this subject was by Dr. Kenneth Doyle, a financial psychologist at the University of Minnesota. Dr. Doyle concluded from his studies that there are four basic "money languages" people speak.

The Driver—Money is success

To this group of people, money protects against the fear of incompetence. The more money they have, the more competent they feel.

"Drivers" communicate love by showing what money has done to bless and improve the lives of those around them—houses, cars, clothing, and so on.

The weakness of this money language is that "Drivers" can be overly dependent upon money for their self-esteem and significance. Rather than trust God and focus on the eternal values of life, "Drivers" tend to be more materialistic and greedy.

The Analytic—Money is security

Money for this group of people wards off chaos and problems. They are the "Analytics," and they are well-structured financially. They are good long-range money planners.

"Analytics" communicate love by saving money and looking out for the future well-being and interests of those they care about.

The weakness of this money language is that "Analytics" can be legalistic and unyielding regarding budgeting and money issues. It's common for people who are around "Analytics" to feel that they are less important than money. "Analytics" can—unintentionally—communicate insensitivity and disregard for the feelings of others because of their conservative financial attitudes.

The Amiable—Money is love

Relationships and people are the focus of the financial desires of "Amiables." Money means love and affection to them. The lack of money translates as an inability to demonstrate love. "Amiables" communicate love by sharing what they have with those around them, especially close family and friends.

The weakness of this money language is that "Amiables" may be generous and good-hearted, but they are often poor money managers with little or no financial structure, or long-range planning.

The Expressive—Money is acceptance

Money for the "Expressives" purchases the respect and admiration of others. Money means acceptance. It provides a basis of relationship with desirable people.

"Expressives" communicate love by shopping, purchasing and spending to please those by whom they desire to be accepted.

The weakness of this money language is that "Expressives" can use money the way some people use alcohol or drugs—to hide feelings of pain, insecurity or incompetence. Rather than relying on God, "Expressives" can be overly dependent on money to solve their problems and calm their fears.

Do you speak any of these four money languages?

What about your spouse?

Do you and your spouse speak the same language, or different languages?

Most people immediately recognize themselves and their spouses in one of these four money languages. What's more, most husbands and wives speak different money languages.

For example, I am an "Amiable" and Karen is an "Analytic." That's why we had so many problems earlier in our marriage. When Karen accused me of being a spendthrift, I accused her of being a tightwad. Neither of us was being malicious. We were just expressing the different ways we viewed money and what it symbolized to us.

In our ignorance, however, we both thought each other's financial input was illegitimate and wrong. In thinking that, there was a constant tug of war over financial issues as we both tried pulling each other from what we perceived was an unhealthy extreme.

Money Problems and Financial Disagreements

But we've changed. Today, Karen and I accept the fact that we are genuinely different, and that is the way God made us. Consequently, we are able to stop judging each other and relax in the understanding that we are different...and it's normal.

Karen and I also have come to understand that we *need* each other. As we realized the legitimacy of our differences, we also acknowledged that we each bring strengths and weaknesses to our "money language."

For instance, I know I need Karen to help me slow down in making money decisions and to have a plan for the future. In turn, Karen knows that I help her "live for today" and not feel guilty about enjoying God's financial blessings.

Karen and I truly are a good team. We make great decisions when we honor each other and admit our need for the other's input and balance—and that's a far cry from where we used to be.

Now, maybe you don't relate to the problems of having different money languages because you and your spouse share the same financial perspective. Beware. Even though you and your spouse may argue less, realize that because you speak the same money language, you also have the same weaknesses and financial blind spots. In fact, it would be a good idea for you both to consider getting outside input on major financial decisions and planning so you can get the balance and perspective you are lacking from each other.

Understanding your financial languages can help stop fights over money and actually lead to healthy discussions. It can also help you appreciate the fact that what you may have been interpreting as a financial weakness in your spouse could have been their effort to express love to you.

No One-Sided Decisions

God created marriage to be a partnership between two equals. Navigating and experiencing life together is the truest pleasure of marriage.

A dominating and controlling husband or wife can rob a marriage of its pleasure as he or she seizes the assets of the covenant union and refuses to receive input or be influenced. In short, dominance by a spouse is destructive to the integrity and intimacy of a marriage relationship.

When speaking of financial dominance, I'm not saying there is anything wrong with delegating certain duties to either spouse. As long as they both have input into the areas they desire, it is usually necessary for one spouse to balance the checkbook or pay the bills. That is not dominance.

Rather, dominance is an attitude of disrespect and solitary control. It manifests itself through a disproportionate control of the assets of the relationship.

Typically, dominance includes many or all areas of a relationship. In the realm of finances, however, it becomes particularly demoralizing and destructive to the spouse being dominated.

I'll never forget receiving a *HELP!* call one night. The wife was ready to walk out, and I was called in to intervene. When I arrived at the couple's house, the wife was sitting in the living room silently. She looked like she had been in a train wreck.

As I began talking with her about why she wanted to leave her husband, I learned that in their more than 30 years of marriage, her husband had totally controlled her. He controlled their home, their money, their children—everything.

Because this woman did not work outside of the home, she was completely dependent upon her husband financially. He had given her tiny amounts of money throughout the course of their marriage, but only after she would beg for it and do everything he demanded in the exact manner he wanted it done.

In the truest sense, this husband completely controlled his wife and his family through money. He gave his wife no checkbook, no credit cards, and he even refused to give her any information as to how much money they had or where it was. As far as she knew, they lived "hand to mouth" and were barely making it. But that was far from the truth.

The wife happened to find a bank statement her husband had not put away. On the statement she discovered that they had, in fact, hundreds of thousands of dollars in one savings account alone. With that, she finally exploded.

As I spoke with her that night, I became sympathetic to her feelings and told her I could understand why she was so resentful.

As I said that, her husband overheard it and corrected me.

"Jimmy, are you telling my wife that leaving me is OK?"

"If I were in her place," I said, "I would have left long ago. I'm surprised she stayed around this long. You have dominated and controlled your wife and everything in this home, and you have no right to do that. I'm not advising her to leave you, but I'm telling you that if you don't change, you have no chance of keeping her here, and I'm not going to try to make her stay."

The husband did not appreciate my comments, to say the least. Yet, their marriage was saved because they ended up going for marriage counseling and he began treating his wife as an equal.

> **Christ-like leadership means that a man is responsible for initiating the well-being of the home. But he is never to dominate his wife.**

Some men think they have a right to dominate the finances of the home by virtue of their being "the head of the home." That's rubbish.

True authority is selfless and sacrificial. That's the model of Christ-like love revealed to us by the Apostle Paul in Ephesians 5. Men are commanded to sacrifice for their wives as they nourish and cherish them.

Christ-like leadership means that a man is responsible for initiating the well-being of the home. But he is never to dominate his wife.

Every woman I know desires her husband to be a loving initiator of the finances, children, spirituality and romance. But no woman wants to be dominated.

Gentlemen, dominating your wife is against God's design, and it destroys the intimacy and trust of marriage.

Dominance Knows No Gender

Ladies, don't be deceived into thinking that men are the only ones who can be guilty of dominating the finances at home. Women can be just as controlling when it comes to money.

Typically, women who "control" the money do not trust their husbands financially. And it's usually for one of two reasons.

The first reason is, when a woman judges her husband's money skills as deficient and believes her financial abilities are superior, she will often do everything she can to guide the financial decisions.

The second reason is, if a woman believes her husband represents a danger to the financial well-being of their home, she will usually try to protect the finances from him.

The truth is, anytime a spouse begins to control the money, problems are going to begin. But if one spouse is truly out of control in the area of money, then the other needs to intervene to try and keep his or her spouse from self-destruction, or from destroying the family.

I once knew of a couple in this situation. The husband had a gambling addiction and ruined the family financially on a number of occasions. Because of his problem, he needed parameters put on him to force him to acknowledge his addiction and to protect their finances. If he had refused to deal with these issues, then separation—not divorce—would have been my recommendation to his wife to protect her and the children from his destructive behavior.

Intervening when a person is truly destructive isn't dominance—it is prudence. Even then, however, it is vital to communicate love to the spouse with the problem and to express that the intention is to help, not to dominate.

> **For you and your spouse truly to become "one" in marriage, you must surrender your individual control for the idea of shared control.**

In these types of severe circumstances, I believe it is always helpful for a couple to go for outside counseling. Even if the destructive spouse won't go, the person trying to redeem the relationship needs support and counsel.

Maybe your spouse isn't destructive, but just different or not perfect. Trying to protect money by hiding it, or refusing to receive your spouse's input will only devastate your relationship.

Again, if you and your spouse don't seem able to solve your problems, then go to a pastor, church leader, Christian counselor or financial advisor. Find someone both of you respect. Then agree beforehand that you will take his or her advice.

Seeking help in times of financial impasse can save your marriage if you will commit to not allowing chronic financial arguments to come between you. Do everything you can to solve the issues as quickly as you can.

I have mentioned in other chapters the superb research on marriage by Dr. John Gottman at the University of Washington.

In one study, Dr. Gottman followed 130 newly married couples over a period of five years. After having observed these couples closely, Dr. Gottman concluded that the common trait among the most successful couples was shared control of the relationship.

In other words, successful couples received input and influence from one another. Where dominance existed, however, the satisfaction of the marriage decreased significantly.

Finally, another common attitude that feeds destructive dominance in money issues is the "my money" mentality. Some people believe that because they owned something before marriage, or because the money came from *their* job, they have the right to control it without the input of their spouses. Again, that's rubbish.

God says, "*...they shall become one...*" (Genesis 2:24).

For you and your spouse truly to become "one" in marriage, you must surrender your individual control for the idea of shared control.

The Apostle Paul takes it a step further in 1 Corinthians 7, by telling us that when we marry, we must share control of our bodies with our spouses for the purpose of them getting their physical needs met.

Marriage definitely was not designed for selfish people. Because, at the core of marriage is a demand of surrender, servanthood and selflessness.

The picture of a perfect marriage is two servants in love.

The picture of a nightmare marriage is two selfish people getting married.

With their "pre-nup" agreement already in hand, these "politically correct" people think they can keep their individuality untouched, yet succeed in marriage.

That is the deception destroying people's hopes of happiness in marriage, today. We extol selfishness as a virtue, yet wonder why we cannot stay married.

Regardless of how long we've owned something or whose job provided the income, everything in marriage must be surrendered to the ownership and influence of our spouses.

Anything we will not surrender to them and receive influence concerning will damage, if not destroy, the intimacy of the marriage.

Remember, intimacy is created by sharing. To the degree we will not share is to the same degree that intimacy will elude us.

> **The picture of a perfect marriage is two servants in love.**
>
> **The picture of a nightmare marriage is two selfish people getting married. With their "pre-nup" agreement already in hand, these "politically correct" people think they can keep their individuality untouched, yet succeed in marriage.**

Get a Plan—Work the Plan

Throughout the Old and New Testaments, the Bible points to one important truth—we must agree if we are going to succeed.

In Luke 11:17, Jesus said that a house divided against itself cannot stand.

Amos 3:3 asks the question, "Can two walk together unless they agree?"

When you and your spouse do not agree about the finances of your home, your financial house cannot stand. It will fall.

One of the longest journeys in life is marriage—at least, that's how it is supposed to be. But when a husband and wife are out of sync with each other and going in different directions, it gets old fast. You must agree before you can journey together successfully.

Proverbs 29:18 would add to that, if you don't have "revelation" or "vision," you will "cast off restraint." That literally means when a couple does not have a clear sense of where they're going, they will not be able to stay together, or to restrain negative behavior.

Many couples fight about money because they constantly react to issues that are happening *today*, rather than being proactive and deciding issues in advance.

To avoid those money fights, you must budget...budget...budget. Making a budget for your household is a critical discipline that helps you talk through difficult financial decisions and come to an agreement. Budgeting can benefit you and your spouse by disarming any feelings of anxiety or tension. Budgeting forces you to discuss the higher values and priorities you have for your lives and marriage. Not having a budget can result in a constant tug of war as you both try to decide what is most important and who gets their way.

A budget also provides a basis of accountability and reproach. If it's "in the budget," you're playing by the rules if you spend the agreed-upon amount. If it's not in the budget and you spend it, you're breaking the rules that you both agreed upon. Without a budget, however, there are no rules. You have to make them up as you go along. And we all know that doesn't work in Monopoly or any other game without causing fights.

Finally, financial conflict is more manageable if you do it when the issues are not so pressing and intense. Granted, preparing a budget—and living by it—can actually cause you to disagree and even argue. But that's OK. It's better to decide to argue and to commit to work it out than it is not to make a budget because it might start an argument that can lead to a running disagreement for the next 40 years.

> Budgeting is simply deciding to "argue" in a healthy setting where you can talk things through and reach a point of agreement. When you're finished, you stop fighting.

Budgeting is simply deciding to "argue" in a healthy setting where you can talk things through and reach a point of agreement. When you're finished, you stop fighting.

Remember, without a budget that you and your spouse can agree upon and commit to, your financial house cannot stand. Your marriage will be constantly plagued by arguments over which way is right and who is going to lead. So, consider praying together and asking God to give you a sense of vision and revelation about His financial will for your marriage. His plan for your lives and your marriage includes your everyday financial needs.

When you receive God's will and commit to it, it will take your marriage to a glorious level of intimacy, agreement and blessing. Karen and I have experienced this personally, and it is awesome.

Decide today to begin the process of preparing a budget if you don't already have one. If you need help, there are a lot of great computer programs, as well as terrific resources specifically designed for couples from Christian financial experts such as Larry Burkett.

The point is, start seeking God *together* and ask Him to give you wisdom and direction.

Avoid Debt at All Cost

Proverbs 22:7 tells us, *"The rich rules over the poor, and the borrower is servant to the lender."*

While I don't believe that means we cannot borrow, it does caution us against the bondage of debt that results from ignorance in the financial realm.

Couples who fight about finances are often over their heads in debt. They have credit cards charged to their limit, but are only making the minimum payment. So, they're paying extremely high interest payments every month.

On top of that, most couples have mortgage debt, car loans and other forms of debt. When the debt payments that are due each month challenge or exceed their ability to pay them, tremendous stress is put on their marriage.

As the stress of debt intensifies, frustrated husbands and wives usually begin pointing their fingers at each other and blaming one another for their debts and financial pressures. The longer that scenario continues, the more stress it puts on the marriage and the higher the risk of serious problems between them becomes.

To avoid the pitfalls of debt overload, here are some steps I recommend you take to solve the problems you face today and help prevent others in the future:

Don't owe God.

Malachi 3 commands us to tithe, which means to give the first 10 percent of our income to God.

When I first heard this, I thought it was insane. Through Karen's faith and encouragement, however, we tried it. The year we began giving to the Lord, our total income was around $7,000 and we had a one-year-old child. In spite of my unbelief, when we began to give, God began doing miracles in our finances.

He'll do the same for you.

According to the Bible, when you don't tithe, you are robbing God, and you place yourself in debt to Him. While you're in that condition, He will not bless you.

But if you will give to God faithfully, He promises that He will "open the windows of heaven" and pour out His blessings.

Since that time years ago, Karen and I have continued to give. Consequently, we live in God's blessings.

So, don't be in debt to God. Pay Him first and recognize His authority in the area of your finances. That puts God on your side financially and prepares you for lasting financial security and success.

Save and live within your means.

If you are not saving money regularly, you are not living within your means.

Also, if you are not saving, you have no ability to deal with the inevitable unexpected expenses of life. Therefore, you live in constant stress and become even more dependent upon debt.

Living within your means is establishing a lifestyle that allows you to give to the Lord, save money regularly and pay for the essentials of life—house, utilities, food and the like—without going into debt...or getting under stress. If you cannot do this, you have established an unaffordable lifestyle.

Using debt to finance an unaffordable lifestyle is a short-term fix with serious long-term consequences.

The opposite is true of saving and living within your means.

Because you are willing to be content with less and delay gratification, you may not have as much, but you are able to enjoy it and each other without stress.

Also, the longer you save and live within your means, the more you are able to afford what you desire without debt. Therefore, you get what you want without stress or binding debt.

For many people who are in debt, the answer is *downsize*. Perhaps you need to move into a smaller home or drive an older automobile. Whatever you must do to be able to save and live within your means, it will be worth it to relieve stress and put you into a successful pattern of life.

When people are absolutely unwilling to consider downsizing and making the necessary—though difficult—choices to delay gratification, it is usually because a spirit of greed, covetousness and materialism is controlling them. Experience will reveal these are harsh taskmasters that are never satisfied.

Selling your soul for material possessions is a deceptive and dangerous way to live. It is a sin to be controlled by material things and not God.

Some people justify their financially driven lifestyle by the "we're-doing-it-for-our-children" line.

What your children need most is to live in a peace-filled home with parents who love each other and to know they are loved. Of course, you want to be good providers for your children, but what is enough? Do they really need everything their friends have? Can material possessions replace the time they need with you, or make up for the fights they hear you and your spouse having that produce anxiety and fear within them?

The most important things in life are free. The things that have to be

> **Some people justify their financially driven lifestyle by the "we're-doing-it-for-our-children" line. What your children need most is to live in a peace-filled home with parents who love each other amd to know they are loved.**

purchased may be necessary, but they cannot produce love, peace or happiness. If they could, all rich people would be happy. But they're not.

Borrow wisely and cautiously.

If you are going to borrow money, make sure you can service the debt without compromising yourselves financially. Also, don't borrow for highly depreciating or perishable items such as vacations, eating out, groceries and gasoline.

I know people who buy perishable and consumable items such as groceries on a credit card and then pay the minimum payment every month. When their credit card hits the maximum, they continue to pay the minimum payment and apply for a new card. That is financial insanity.

Credit card interest is the highest you can pay. If you use a credit card, discipline yourself to pay it off at the end of every month. If you have credit card debt, prioritize it as the first you pay off.

Living on credit card debt is not living—it's existing. And the longer you do it, the more stressful and unhappy your existence becomes.

I realized long ago that whatever joy I receive by purchasing something I cannot afford is long forgotten by the pain of having to pay it off. What's even worse is when you're still paying for something you consumed long ago.

Borrowing money for homes, cars or things like that can be prudent in some situations. But that doesn't mean we wouldn't rather pay cash if we could. It just means these are essential items that we need and can justify borrowing for as long as it is within our means. Even then, shop for the best interest rates and pay the debt off as quickly as possible to keep from paying unnecessary interest.

Get financial advice and input.

The wealthiest people I know are the most teachable in the area of finances. They are the ones who most often hire financial advisors to help them.

On the other hand, the people I know who struggle the most in the area of their finances struggle because they are often threatened by any outside input and will not seek help.

I openly admit that financial management is not my strongest gift. That's why I'm glad I have gifted people around me who help me in this area. God has gifted some people with financial wisdom, and the rest of us need to receive their input.

If you are in serious debt and are having problems financially, get help. Don't try to solve all your problems on your own. If you cannot afford to pay for financial advice, there are some wonderful non-profit consumer debt agencies that help people deal with creditors as they work their way out of financial problems. Many churches offer financial counseling and help.

So, don't be stubborn or proud. Be teachable and admit your weaknesses. That's the attitude of the individuals and couples I know who have overcome adversity and have achieved financial unity and success.

God wants your marriage to be an oasis of blessing and intimacy. And let's face it, financial blessing is one of the greatest joys of life. If you will respect your spouse, walk in unity and avoid debt, then you can enjoy the blessings of marriage and money the way God intended.

Chapter Six

Resolving the Stress of
Sexual Problems and Unmet Sexual Needs

One of the most important features of marriage is sexual fulfillment. Sexual attraction, after all, is a primary factor that causes couples to fall in love and get married.

But long after the honeymoon is over, husbands and wives need to do everything they can to maintain a lifelong sexual flow between them, because it is that flow that helps to bond their relationship and increase their level of intimacy.

When the flow of giving and receiving sexual pleasure is broken in a marriage, however, that's when *stress* can enter into the relationship and begin its disastrous work. Whether the interruption to a couple's sexual flow is due to sickness, travel or relationship problems, unmet sexual needs will always pose a threat to the marriage.

That's why in 1 Corinthians 7, the Apostle Paul warns husbands and wives not to withhold their bodies from one another. Doing so gives the devil an opportunity to damage their relationship. Satan's scheme has always been to divide spouses from each other, and then tempt them to go outside the marriage for illicit sexual satisfaction and emotional gratification.

Marriage is a unique relationship that has the potential to fulfill us like nothing else on this earth can. But when the "well" of marriage that's supposed to satisfy our emotional and physical thirst dries up, the complexion of the relationship changes. The longer we live with unmet sexual needs, the greater our level of stress and anxiety will become.

It's the X-Y Chromosome Thing

I have found there to be three key issues that affect sexual fulfillment in marriage. If we understand these issues, I believe we can disarm the common problems that create sexual tension and stress in marriage.

The first of these is the age-old issue—boys are different than girls.

In 1999, the *Journal of the American Medical Association* reported that the primary problem for women was lack of sexual desire. For men, the primary problem was premature ejaculation. The article was another confirmation that men and women are different, particularly when it comes to sexuality.

When Karen and I first got married, I was completely ignorant concerning the inherent sexual differences between us. What's more, I had been deceived by years of pornography, locker room lies and media portrayals of sex. In short, I was a sexual problem going somewhere to happen.

Consequently, when Karen and I married, though we were attracted to each other and had an active sex life, we both had a lot of frustration due to wrong sexual expectations. It took us years to understand our differences and to begin to respect them.

As Karen and I grew in our understanding and respect for each other's differences, however, our sexual intimacy and pleasure increased dramatically. We no longer had unrealistic expectations of one another. We didn't expect each other to act in a way that was outside of our nature. Basically, we each got the revelation that I was a man and she was a woman—and that meant we were different.

Part of this revelation Karen and I received was the realization that men and women are different when it comes to being stimulated sexually.

Men are visually stimulated, and women are emotionally stimulated.

Women are by no means blind when it comes to sex, but they do have a much greater capacity for responding to emotional stimulation. And that's hard for men to understand.

Men typically do not take enough time to talk to their wives and patiently meet their emotional and romantic needs. That lack of emotional support for their wives costs men dearly when it comes to sex.

Men, realize that your wife is not going to "turn on" sexually just because you take your clothes off. Your wife will really only "turn on" because you talk to her throughout the day and pay attention to her. The reason is, your wife can rarely respond to sex beyond the state of her emotions. That doesn't mean she cannot give herself to you sexually if she doesn't feel like it. It simply means that *her* sexuality is directly tied into her emotional nature.

God made women this way because He is concerned about the overall integrity of the relationship, not just about sex. He designed sex—within marriage—to reach its potential only if genuine care and sensitivity are present.

Sadly, the opposite is the more common scenario: A selfish husband ignoring his wife until bedtime, and then expecting his emotionally impoverished wife to perform sexually.

But in His divine genius, God created a system that ensures jerks don't get the best sex.

No, the best sex in the world is only achieved by respecting the differences in our spouses. For a man, that means caring for his wife in a sensitive and sacrificial manner. That includes the all-important ingredient of romance.

Husbands, romance is simply your being the initiator. Pursue your wife. But pursue her and seek to please her on her level of need and desire, not yours. When you do that, your wife will open up to you sexually and respond to you every time.

For a woman, respecting the differences in her husband means realizing that he gets sexually aroused by simply looking at her naked body. The problem is, because women are not as visually stimulated as men and because they are more critical of their bodies, they tend to discount this real need in their husbands and thereby frustrate them.

> **To understand the sexual differences between men and women, all you have to do is look at how they sin. Men turn to pornography, which wrongfully feeds their visual needs. Women turn to soap operas and romance novels, which wrongfully fulfill their emotional needs.**

Ladies, your husband wants to *see* your body. And while flannel nightgowns worn in a pitch-black bedroom are a sexual refuge for many of you—all in the name of not "exposing" yourself—they are the archenemy of sexual fulfillment for your husband.

Just as a man needs to understand and meet his wife's *emotional* needs, a woman must respect and fulfill her husband's *visual* needs. And oftentimes that means going outside of her comfort zone to wear attractive lingerie before sex and expose her body to her husband before and during sex.

To understand the sexual differences between men and women, all you have to do is look at how they sin. Men turn to pornography, which wrongfully feeds their visual needs. Women turn to soap operas and romance novels, which wrongfully fulfill their emotional needs.

The bottom line is, don't pursue sexual fulfillment outside your marriage. That's sin. Instead, learn to respect your spouse's differences and meet his or her needs.

Another important difference that Karen and I learned about men and women in our marriage is that men need sexual touching and women need non-sexual affection.

I have to admit that this is one of the most confusing differences between the sexes. Yet, when we don't grasp this fundamental difference, sex becomes a bittersweet battle of wills.

Here's a common scenario played out in countless bedrooms: An aggressive husband roughly gropes for his wife's genitals as she complains and then retreats into a sexually defensive posture. The result is that their needs are denied and they both end up frustrated.

Sound familiar?

A woman has a deep need for soft, non-sexual touching throughout the day, as well as during sex. It makes her feel valued and emotionally cared for. In fact, the more soft, non-sexual affection a man gives his wife, the more sexually responsive she becomes.

But, again, that's just the opposite of the way a man is designed and thinks. Most men think the way to arouse their wives is the way they are turned on—by direct sexual touching. That's not the case, however, and it will only lead to a woman's sexual frustration.

Now, obviously, a woman needs direct stimulation to her clitoris to be able to reach orgasm. But that, too, must be done in a tender, gentle manner that satisfies her desire and does not ignore her overall need for soft, non-sexual affection.

In contrast, a woman needs to understand that her husband desires—and needs—touches that are directly sexual. It is very satisfying and stimulating for a man, and it meets a deep need in him.

So, when couples understand each other and respect their differing natures, their times of intimacy will involve an affectionate husband caressing and gently touching his wife...and a wife touching her husband's penis and other areas of his body that sexually stimulate him.

The most dangerous element that threatens sexual fulfillment and creates destructive stress in a marriage is selfishness. Refusing to accept each other's sexual differences ensures that both will be left frustrated and unfulfilled.

The best sex is achieved when a husband and wife are working to meet each other's needs. Two sensitive and selfless people are the ones who reach sexual fulfillment in their marriage.

The other male-female difference that Karen and I came to understand is that men and women have different levels of sexual need, and they achieve orgasms differently.

Most men are more sexual than their wives. They think about sex more and have a more intense need for it more often. That's especially true among younger men between 18 and 45 years of age. But that usually begins to change as men age. As they move into their 40s and 50s, their testosterone level gradually drops, which causes a decrease in sexual desire.

As women age, however, their desire for sex often increases. That's due, in part, to an increased emotional security in their marriages. Likewise, the absence of the fear of pregnancy as well as a greater acceptance of their sexuality can cause women to become more open sexually.

The point is, throughout the life of a marriage, it's possible for either spouse to desire sex more often, less often, or the same amount as the other. Seldom will their desires be exactly the same. And while it is typically the man who desires sex more than his wife, I have counseled many a frustrated wife whose husband was not interested in sex.

So, we need to be accepting of each other, even though we don't always have the same sexual intensity or need at the same time. It is devastating for a husband or a wife to be judged, ignored, or rejected by a spouse when expressing a sexual need.

> **Throughout the life of a marriage, it's possible for either spouse to desire sex more often, less often, or the same amount as the other. Seldom will their desires be exactly the same.**

Now, when it comes to the fulfillment of all these *needs*—sexual orgasms—it's important to understand the "mechanics" behind it all.

To begin with, a man must achieve orgasm to experience sexual fulfillment.

In contrast, a woman can have sex with her husband without experiencing an orgasm and still be very satisfied. But while that is true, most women desire orgasms on a regular basis.

Men almost always achieve orgasm during intercourse. Women rarely do.

Though a woman can have an orgasm during intercourse, it's usually difficult because a woman's primary sexual organ that produces an orgasm is her clitoris, which is located outside and above her vagina. Her clitoris needs to be stimulated for her to have an orgasm. So, she needs to help her husband by guiding him to stimulate her properly...the way she likes it.

For most men, *Slow down!* is the key to their wives having orgasms. But men also need to be gentle and listen to their wives. Again, men can selfishly rush into sex and only care about getting their own needs met. That only results in a wife feeling used and sexually frustrated. The challenge for men is that they can become sexually aroused almost instantly. Consequently, they tend to rush their wives into a sexual response that they are unable to give without the proper care.

So, husbands, understand that your wife warms up to sex much more slowly than you do. She needs your attention *before, during,* and *after* sex, in order to experience complete fulfillment.

Now, granted, some sex in marriage can be satisfying through what is commonly called *quickies.* And usually it's the wife who offers her body to her husband for the sake of meeting an immediate sexual need. Intercourse is brief and more spontaneous.

But, remember, husbands, "quickies" are not going to cut it for your wife. She needs your attention. She needs to be romanced and cared for long before sex. During sex, listen to her...she will tell you what she needs. That is the only way she can ever reach an orgasm and be fully satisfied.

So, understanding all these differences between men and women, and respecting your spouse's sexual nature will help you disarm destructive stress and lead you both to sexual fulfillment like you've never known it before.

Get Rid of the Problems

If you and your spouse want to experience sexual satisfaction for a lifetime, you need to be prepared to combat some common problems that are out to sabotage your sexual fulfillment.

One of these problems is anger—specifically, *unresolved* anger as I described in Chapter 3. Anger is inevitable in every marriage. There's no way two people can live together without becoming angry at each other at some point. Even the healthiest of couples can experience anger on a regular basis.

So, the issue in marriage is not, *Will we experience anger?*

The issue is, *How do we deal with it?*

In men and women, there is a direct connection between emotions and sexual responses.

When we resolve issues in our marriages successfully, our sex lives are unhindered as we express our physical love. It's when those issues remain unresolved and anger builds that our sexual desires and responses change.

Personally, I believe unresolved anger is the most dangerous element in marriage.

Earlier in this book, I addressed in detail how to resolve anger. And as I said then, anger is like toxic waste that cannot be stored inside us without causing damage. It must be dealt with quickly to avoid any harm in our relationships.

In Ephesians 4:26, the Apostle Paul tells us to admit our anger, but not let the sun go down on it.

Good sex actually increases the emotional temperature of the marriage and builds feelings of intimacy and goodwill.

In this case, our sexual health is not just a matter of how our bodies respond to sexual stimuli. It is very much dependent upon our emotional state. And unresolved anger means that there are feelings of hurt, mistrust, or violation between a husband and wife. The more these negative feelings accumulate and remain unresolved the more they will affect their sexual responses to one another.

In reality, sex is like a thermometer and thermostat in a marriage.

As a thermostat, sex makes marriage better. Good sex actually increases the emotional temperature of the marriage and builds feelings of intimacy and goodwill.

But sex also acts as a thermometer, which means it reflects the state of the relationship. And a lack of healthy sexual exchange between a couple for any significant length of time is a warning signal that must be heeded.

If you have any unresolved anger in your marriage, I recommend you and your spouse be honest with yourselves and each other. Discuss your feelings. Commit to forgive each other and not to allow anger and bitterness to exist between you.

If you find there is an issue, or issues, you cannot resolve, get counseling from a Christian leader or professional. Your marriage is too important to allow problems to remain unresolved. It's robbing you both of the intimacy and pleasure every married couple can and should experience.

In our fast-paced culture, it's no surprise that *stress* is another familiar issue that's forever trying to rob marriages of intimacy and sexual fulfillment.

The demands of jobs, children, housework, finances, and so forth often leave one or both spouses exhausted and sexually unresponsive.

If *stress* is not a frequent issue in your household, then it's not a problem. It's when stress becomes a frequent guest in your home that it can create deep frustration for one or both spouses, because sexual needs are being ignored.

As I said earlier, the first thing we must do to remove stress from our lives is to prioritize. None of us can "have it all." So, life must be prioritized to be successful. And those priorities must be protected from competing demands.

It's important, even necessary, that you and your spouse take an inventory of your lives on a regular basis, especially when you are experiencing stress. Examine those things that are physically, mentally and emotionally demanding.

If you find that your greater priorities—God, your spouse and your children—are being robbed of their rightful place by lesser priorities such as friends, work, sports, hobbies and entertainment, then reprioritize and remove some of the lesser.

Earlier in our marriage, I gave up golf for several years for this very reason. I have always loved to play golf, but at that time it was an idol. I would go directly from work to the golf course and then come home exhausted and unwilling to meet Karen's needs. Yet, I expected her to serve me and meet my sexual needs.

> **The first thing we must do to remove stress from our lives is to prioritize.**

Karen became deeply resentful. It became a major issue in our marriage. So, I reprioritized.

I have to admit that giving up golf was a sacrifice for me, but it was a small price to pay for the wonderful intimacy and sexual pleasure Karen and I have enjoyed since.

Now, along those lines, I would also suggest to any husband wanting good sex, take responsibility in helping your wife with the kids and the home.

It is unfair for a man to come home from work and sit in front of the television, and expect his wife to bear the burden of the children and housework—and then, after she goes to bed exhausted, be willing and able to meet his sexual needs energetically.

Whether a wife works outside of the home or full-time at home, a husband needs to let her know that he is her partner in every area of life. A wise husband who wants to enjoy good sex will help bear the burdens for his wife and allow her to have a time of rest and relaxation before sex. An unwise husband will ignore his wife and refuse to accept responsibility for the home, children, finances, or other issues causing her stress.

In dealing with these common stresses of life, it's good to plan sex in advance. While planning times of intimacy in advance is not intended to prevent spontaneous sex, it does help secure a special date for sex on a regular basis so a husband and wife can each prepare properly.

When our children were young and we had many demands on us, this is what Karen and I did. We would decide in advance to have an evening together, and we made every sacrifice necessary for it to happen. These were always great times for us because we prioritized and planned for them. Also, every two or three months, we would go for a night or two to a motel or hotel, just to be alone together.

When I look back on our marriage and how we succeeded in very busy times, I believe this was a key reason. We didn't let circumstances dictate our sexual relationship. We made our times of being together and enjoying sex a top priority. We made it happen.

One final problem that is common among marriages today, and must be dealt with head-on, is sexual deception.

Take a good look around and it doesn't take long to realize that our world is full of sexual deception. We are surrounded by it.

For men, this deception comes in the form of pornography. Nowadays, a man doesn't have to leave his home to be confronted daily with erotic images. Television, magazines, computers and movies—pornography in one form or another is everywhere.

Pornography is Satan's special weapon to destroy men and marriage. It's nothing less than satanic sex education.

Pornography portrays women as sex objects without emotional needs. Consequently, a man is led to believe that "normal" women want sex as much as he does and in exactly the same way he does. That's what inevitably leads a man to believe that there is something wrong with his wife and that he is being cheated. The more pornography a man views, the more he must see to satisfy the ever-increasing desire it creates. It also has to become raunchier in order to satisfy.

A man's addiction to pornography will eventually reach a level where he wants to act out what he is seeing. And, oftentimes, he will try to use his wife to act it out, which dehumanizes her and makes her nothing less than an object of vaginal masturbation for him. Worse, still, he will go outside the marriage to try and experience the lie of pornography.

Pornography is Satan's special weapon to destroy men and marriage. It's nothing less than satanic sex education.

God designed sex to be satisfying, but only if it includes intimacy. Intimacy is inner closeness and depth of relationship that includes body, soul and spirit. Therefore, sex in marriage is the *only* sex that can satisfy because it draws from all of our experiences and areas of life.

Pornography, on the other hand, bypasses every other area of life and promises sexual fulfillment solely on a physical level. That is the essence of pornography's lie.

I have known men who have destroyed their lives in the pursuit of illicit sexual pleasure. They were constantly driven to feed the monster of sexual excitement, but with ever-diminishing levels of satisfaction. They abused and abandoned their wives as a direct result of the deception of pornography.

Men, however, are not the only ones vulnerable to sexual deception.

For women, that deception comes in the form of romance novels, soap operas, movies and female erotica. These court a woman's differing sexual temperament—and as with pornography, they are all forms of satanic sex education.

For example, romance novels are almost always written by women, for women. They portray reality in the opposite manner as male-oriented pornography. They excite women by downplaying the sexual nature of men and "over-emotionalizing" them. Because these novels are written by women, for women, they typically swing to the sexual perspective of women and ignore the reality of the sexual intensity of men.

The end result of these romance novels, as well as female erotica, is that they convince women that there really are men "out there"—unlike their husbands—who are much more emotional and much less sexual. They deeply implant a deceived perspective in women that many times causes them to judge and reject their husbands as they convince themselves they are losing out on "true love."

To overcome these rampant deceptions in modern society, husbands and wives must reject the devil's lies and refuse to be entertained or excited by them, while understanding the truth about sex.

Sex can only be truly fulfilling as you and your spouse turn your hearts to each other and work hard to meet each other's differing, though valid, needs.

Indeed, you were both created to be different. Yet, great damage is done if you reject those differences and try to conform your spouse into your image.

An Atmosphere of Pleasure

Once you understand the differences between you and your spouse—and how to disarm the common obstacles to sexual fulfillment—you are well on your way to creating an atmosphere of unhindered pleasure, an atmosphere in which you can pursue one of the greatest blessings of life and marriage.

We are sexual beings. And without a doubt, sex is the greatest physical pleasure in life.

Sexual Problems and Unmet Sexual Needs

As I said earlier, God created marriage in a paradise called *Eden*. In fact, the word *Eden* actually means "pleasure and delight." God was making it quite clear to us that His design and desire for our marriages was that they be places of sexual pleasure and delight.

But, while every married couple may engage in sexual intercourse, not every couple experiences the same level or frequency of *pleasure*.

As we close this chapter, I want to propose to you four practical steps you and your spouse can take that can ensure "great sex" in a world of "great stress"—steps that will help you grow your own Garden of Eden, an atmosphere favorable to increased sexual pleasure.

First, give attention to physical health and proper grooming.

There are two dangerous extremes in our society today related to our bodies and sex.

One extreme is the drive for physical perfection, which causes many people to go to unhealthy extremes to try to make themselves more attractive. It also causes them to demand unrealistic physical standards of their spouses.

The other is when people abuse their health without regard to how it affects their spouse and their sexual relationship. Alcohol, drugs, obesity—these physical factors greatly affect your sexuality and your marriage.

So, take responsibility and take care of your body because your sexual performance is directly affected by your health. This is especially true the older you get. Exercise and diet are critical elements to sustaining sexual health in both men and women.

Also, gentlemen, included in the "physical health" side of sex is good grooming. In other words, don't approach your wife with dirty hands and a five o'clock shadow. And while you're at it, trim your nose hair and ear hair, brush your teeth and "clean" your breath. Surprise your wife and dress up now and then, too. Men, if you really want to turn on your wife, simple detail to grooming will do it every time.

And, ladies, if you got all "dolled-up" to catch your man, stay "dolled-up" so you can keep him. You *visually* stimulated him the first time—don't stop.

My second suggestion for creating an atmosphere of sexual pleasure is that you and your spouse communicate honestly and openly with each other about your sexual needs and desires.

The only way you can both truly know how to please each other sexually is for you to communicate what you do and do not like. You can—and should—do this before, during and after sex.

To communicate effectively, however, you must create an atmosphere where you both feel comfortable sharing your sexual needs and desires. You must share—and receive what's being shared—without rejecting or condemning each other.

Now, obviously, if your spouse shares a "desire" that is somehow sinful or violates your conscience, then don't feel obligated to accept it.

Nonetheless, even if it is something that's sinful or violates you, be careful how you respond. It's important that we let our spouses know that we love them and are committed to them sexually. And let me say this: It's especially important for women to be true to their conscience without damaging the relationship with her husband or communicating rejection.

For example, men can become very frustrated when their wives only communicate with them about sex through negatives. Rather than openly share their desires and what pleases them, women tend to reserve their "sexual comments" for when their husbands are doing something wrong.

"Stop—that hurts!"

"Don't do that...I don't like it!"

Too often, those are the only kinds of instructions women give their husbands to guide them in trying to please them. Not only is it frustrating for men, but it's also confusing and counterproductive.

Almost every man I know wants to please his wife sexually. At the same time, however, men need *positive* instruction in order to succeed in doing so. Simply put, ladies, your husband needs a road map to help him get on—and stay on—the road to pleasing you sexually. And you're the one who needs to supply him with that map.

Now, for a lot of people, especially women, their repressive attitudes about sex act as an obstacle to such a road map. Repressive or negative attitudes either come from the environment in which you were raised, or they are the result of past sexual sin.

To overcome such obstacles, it helps to remember that God created sex. Sex is a beautiful gift from God. In fact, His perfect will is that you have a pleasurable and exciting sex life with your spouse.

Obviously, if you've done something wrong in your past, you need to repent and receive God's forgiveness. Don't let the mistakes of your past keep you from succeeding today.

Likewise, if you have been sexually abused at some time in your past, take it to the Lord and allow Him to heal you of that hurt. There's nothing that God cannot heal or give you the power to overcome.

Remember, like anything else, sex can be good or bad. Use your past as a reminder of what you should not do. Let God's Word be your guide of what you should do.

My point is, don't be ashamed of sex or treat it as taboo. Do whatever it takes to get to the place where you can talk about your sexual desires.

Encourage your spouse to do the same. Don't let the devil rob you of the joy of sex by making it a dirty subject.

Sex is God's creation. It is one of the greatest blessings in life—and that's the attitude you should always have about it.

Sex was created by God for two reasons—to procreate and to give pleasure in marriage. The focus of my third suggestion is on the *pleasure* aspect of sex.

Use creativity and energy in giving sexual pleasure to your spouse. It is very important that you and your spouse feel free to explore the realms of sexual pleasure, but know where the boundaries are.

As I've taught and counseled on sex over the years, many people have asked me privately about what is, and is not, "allowed" in sex. Oftentimes, I find couples are reluctant to experiment in their sexuality out of a fear that they will sin, or do something wrong. I frequently get questions about oral sex, anal sex, using vibrators or sex toys, different sexual positions and acting out sexual fantasies.

Again, God wants you and your spouse to enjoy sex. And when something is not specifically forbidden in Scripture, that means it generally is because it's allowed. Take oral sex, for example. I've heard a lot of preachers say that oral sex is sin. Yet, nowhere in the Bible does it say that oral sex is forbidden.

Now, while I am not necessarily endorsing or recommending oral sex, anal sex and so forth, I do not believe a minister—or anyone else for that matter—has the moral authority to tell husbands and wives what they can or cannot do in the privacy of their bedrooms...when the Bible has not forbidden it.

When it comes to deciding what is and is not an appropriate sexual practice, I suggest the following guidelines:

- Is it forbidden in the Bible? (Adultery, pornography, homosexuality, bestiality, sex outside of marriage, incest and pedophilia are forbidden.)
- Does it violate your conscience before God?
- Does it violate your spouse, or is it against his or her will?
- Is it physically safe—does it cause harm to you or your spouse?
- Does it treat your spouse in a disrespectful manner, or damage your relationship?

God wants you and your spouse to have fun and enjoy sex. But there are parameters for sexual fulfillment in marriage. Certainly, if something "feels good" and it is not against God's Word, then consider making it a practice in your marriage.

The best marriages are those in which two people enjoy each other and make each other feel good. So, it's important that husbands and wives approach sex from this perspective and not from the opinions of other people.

You know better than anyone—except God—what you like and what is best for your marriage. When properly practiced, sex will build and bond your relationship and will create an atmosphere of pleasure and delight.

So, once you both know how to resolve questions related to your sexual practices, put energy into pleasing each other.

True sexual fulfillment is experienced when two people are sensitive to one another and are committed to meeting each other's sexual needs in a creative and energetic manner. Never get lazy or take your spouse for granted. Find out what pleases him or her. The more you put into it, the more your marriage will benefit.

If you have not already noticed, there are seasons in every marriage that bring special challenges. Therefore, it is in these especially *trying* times that I suggest you and your spouse commit to finding solutions to any sexual problems that might arise.

After all, the benefits of "great sex" in your marriage are worth it.

Here's an example of what I mean.

When women enter their late 30s and early 40s, the normal lubrication of their vaginas during sex typically begins to dry up. Consequently, sex can become painful. If a solution is not found, a woman can begin to resist the sexual advances of her husband and eventually dread sex.

The solution for this common problem is for a husband to use K-Y Jelly or another water-based lubricant during intercourse or when he stimulates his wife's clitoris. These lubricants replace a woman's natural lubrication and can help restore the pleasure of sex without pain.

For men, a common problem that comes with age is erectile difficulty. This is obviously a problem that requires a solution. With the discovery of drugs such as Viagra that are now on the market, there is no need for any man to not have erections and enjoy good sex for the rest of his life.

Regardless of what challenge you and your spouse might face—fear of becoming pregnant, pregnancy, menopause, a serious illness—it is important that you face it together and that you find a solution.

If a medical issue is involved, consult a physician. If the issues are emotional or spiritual in nature, get whatever help is necessary to keep your marriage as healthy as possible. Keep in mind, whenever you face a challenging time in life, your sexual needs and your spouse's sexual needs do not necessarily go away.

Sex is a constant current that ebbs and flows through your life. Anytime it is stopped for any significant period of time—for any reason—it must be dealt with as a serious problem. Give it your attention. Keep destructive sexual stress from damaging your relationship, and you will ensure that your sexual needs, and your spouse's, will be met for a lifetime.

Chapter Seven

Resolving the Stress of
Parenting and Child
Discipline Problems

The presence of children in our lives brings a joy and fulfillment that is indescribable. Children turn a marriage into a family. They are the miraculous fruit of our love and united lives. And once they are born and put into our arms, we become their guardians and guides.

Consequently, it is marriage that truly provides the foundation to the present security and future potential of children. If a marriage is solid, the children will be blessed. If there are cracks in the foundation of a marriage, the result will be stress for the parents and instability for the children.

Make no mistake, children test the integrity and strength of every marriage. Children are a blessing, but they are also a challenge for even the best of parents.

The challenge for us as parents is to raise our children successfully while maintaining a strong, intimate and healthy marriage. To do one without the other is to end up in failure.

So, while there is definitely some built-in stress when it comes to parenting, the key to your success as a parent is to identify the "damaging" kinds of stress. Whether it's disagreeing over how to discipline the children, problems with children from a previous marriage, or the feeling that one parent is detached from the children, you must identify and deal with the stress.

To help get you started, in this chapter I have identified four common stress points to parenting and I will show you how to disarm them. I also address key principles of parenting that will enable you to succeed in raising great children, *and* maintaining a great marriage.

The Good Cop—Bad Cop Routine

When interrogating suspects, police often use a tactic to get the information they're after. It goes like this: One police officer plays the "bad" guy, while the other officer pretends to be the friend—the "good" guy—and protector of the suspect. When successful, this strategy causes suspects to inadvertently trust the "good" cop and divulge to him the desired information.

While the good cop-bad cop routine may work well in police work, it doesn't work in parenting.

In fact, in many stress-filled homes you are likely to find one parent acting as the loving, fun and permissive "friend" of the children, while the other parent is the strict, responsibility-oriented disciplinarian. In other words, there's a good cop and a bad cop.

There are several reasons why this scenario evolves in a home. The first is guilt.

One parent, usually a father, works a lot or is gone too much, and then comes home and wants to make up for lost time by being fun and loving. He doesn't want to work all day and come home, just to be the "hit man." So, he plays the role of the good cop. This situation is damaging because it puts the burden of discipline, character training and responsibility management on his wife. She ends up becoming the bad cop.

Another reason this pattern develops is the mismatch of personalities between parents and children. Most parents have at least one child with whom they identify more easily and understand better—and one child with whom it is difficult for them to relate.

The natural tendency is for parents to be *easier* on children they understand better and tougher on those they don't. When that happens, the other parent will typically assume the opposite role to make up for the error.

Karen and I faced this in our parenting. While I related easily to our daughter, Julie, Karen related easily to our son, Brent. Therefore, I was tougher on Brent, and Karen was tougher on Julie. We also took up for the child we understood most when we felt the other parent was being too hard on them.

The problem with the good cop-bad cop routine is that children desperately need a balance of love, affection, verbal affirmation and attention from both parents. A combination of same-sex and opposite-sex love and attention is very important to their emotional and sexual development. That's why parents must not allow themselves to become imbalanced toward either extreme of parenting.

When Karen and I realized what we were doing and the problems it was causing between us, we stopped. We worked hard to make sure we were both loving and strict to both children. Our efforts kept us from being divided by our children. In turn, our children didn't grow up with an imbalance of love and affection from their parents.

Parents can also fall into this routine because one or both of them is a codependent parent. They need the approval and emotional support of their children.

When husbands or wives are codependent upon their children, they will usually not discipline them properly for fear of losing the approval of the children. This kind of codependency is very unhealthy.

Because codependent parents typically want to be thought of as "cool" by their children and their children's friends, they often sacrifice long-term character training for short-term emotional gratification. This leaves the other parent to perform discipline and enforce responsibilities on the children.

However the scenario is played out, in the end, the parents become divided and begin playing tug-of-war at the expense of their children, which is abusive and selfish.

If you and your spouse find yourselves parenting in this manner, share your feelings and the realization that you may be at an extreme. Talk it out. Then work to understand each other and agree to demonstrate the same type of affection and discipline to the children.

That's what your children need. And it's the only thing that will keep your marriage solid.

On the other hand, if you are not able to resolve this issue with your spouse, realize that you can do a lot of good on your own simply by taking responsibility for your own mistakes and changing. Don't blame your behavior on your spouse, and don't let fear control you.

Do the right thing. Relate to your children in a healthy way. As you do, it will be good for your children, and it will be the best thing you can do to help your spouse recognize and change any wrong behavior.

Case of the Distracted Parent

A second common point of stress in parenting comes when one or both parents are distracted from their children. Malachi 4:5-6 explains.

"Behold, I will send you Elijah the prophet before the coming of the great and dreadful day of the Lord. And he will turn the hearts of the fathers to the children, and the hearts of the children to their fathers, lest I come and strike the earth with a curse."

Malachi reveals two important aspects about fathers with a distracted heart.

First, the root of the problem is spiritual.

Here, God promises to send a prophet on a spiritual mission to turn the hearts of fathers to their children. Obviously, many men in our nation today need a change of heart. Absent and distracted fathers is one of the root issues causing many problems in our society.

Second, Malachi points out that distracted parenting brings a curse upon a family and a nation. God warns that if the fathers don't turn their hearts to their children, He will smite the earth with a curse.

You don't have to look far to see that curse at work in our nation these days. Drive-by shootings, gangs, school violence, teen suicide, teen alcohol and drug abuse, teen pregnancy—the list goes on and on. These are all directly linked to the lack of involvement of fathers in their children's lives.

Mothers are typically very connected to their children and try to emotionally connect fathers to the needs and condition of the kids. Fathers, on the other hand, have a tendency to place the responsibilities of parenting on their wives, as though raising children were "women's work."

Focusing on themselves and their careers, hobbies, friendships, and so forth, men have a tendency to detach emotionally from their children to pursue interests outside the home. This puts a tremendous strain on women

There is nothing wrong in our country today that caring fathers cannot cure very quickly.

as it creates a spiritual and emotional void in the lives of children, which the mothers will instinctively try to fill in either legitimate or illegitimate ways.

There is nothing wrong in our country today that caring fathers cannot cure very quickly. God spoke the solution through the prophet Malachi.

Now, granted, mothers can get distracted, too. With more women employed outside the home than ever before, distraction is becoming a more common problem among mothers. But, in general, fathers tend to be far more distracted from their children.

That was how I was as a father.

When our children were young, my heart was not truly turned toward them. I loved them. I spent time with them. But I was distracted from them by many things, especially my job.

Karen, meanwhile, was a very attentive and caring mother. When I came home at night, she would immediately begin to try to connect me to the needs of our children. She would recruit my involvement with them, which I resented because I considered it to be controlling and insensitive.

Sadly, at that point in my life, I viewed parenting as primarily a woman's job. I knew the importance of a father in providing an income, protecting the family and enforcing discipline. Yet, I didn't see my role as a nurturer or *present* guide to my children. I thought Karen was supposed to be those.

Consequently, I never had a problem with being away from home a lot. And when I did get home at night, I wanted an enjoyable time with Karen and the children, but I didn't want to assume heavy parenting responsibilities.

Needless to say, this was a great source of tension between Karen and me.

I do remember, however, when all that changed. I was sitting in my office at work. And in an instant of time, my heart *turned* toward my children. I started thinking about them and became very emotional. Suddenly, I felt a deep desire to be with them and to relate to them intimately. I could not wait to get home that day.

With the help of Karen's prayers, God did just as He promised in the book of Malachi—He turned my heart toward my children and rescued our family from the curses that would have resulted from my sin.

Ladies, pray for your husband if his heart is turned away from your children. His heart is the root issue, so ask God to change it. Share your feelings with your husband and let him know what you need from him as a partner in parenting.

Men, if you realize that your heart is not really turned toward your children, ask God to change you. Understand that nothing in life can produce the fulfillment and joy that parenting brings.

Dependence Has Its Limits

All of us are dependent. God made us that way. He especially wants us to depend upon Him in all of life's circumstances. He promises us His love, His power and His provision, if we will pray and trust Him.

Certainly, God alone can meet our deepest needs and provide the ever-present internal and eternal guidance and friendship we require. But beyond our dependence upon Him, we are also dependent upon other people for love,

Codependent parents almost always have unmet emotional needs caused by a lack of intimacy in their marriage.

approval and the fulfillment of certain needs. Healthy dependence is a part of life.

For example, adults need other adults to relate to in an emotional and practical give-and-take. Children depend somewhat on peers, but mostly on parents, family members and authority figures. As children grow up, their relationship with God hopefully deepens as they learn to trust in Him more and more. That's how life should be.

When families become unbalanced, however, that's when *dependence* becomes unhealthy.

As I said earlier, codependent parenting is when parents become emotionally dependent upon their children in an unhealthy way. The parents' dependence keeps them from disciplining their children for fear they will reject them.

Codependent parents almost always have unmet emotional needs caused by a lack of intimacy in their marriage. Parents often reach the point where they tell all their problems to their children because they need their understanding and support. They use their children to fill the emotional emptiness in their lives left by the absence of other healthy relationships.

Eventually, this pattern sets up a dysfunctional marriage and family situation resulting in negative feelings and long-term consequences.

A codependent parent hinders a child from developing properly. Because the parent uses the child as an emotional prop, the child is then unable to have a healthy dependence upon that parent. In fact, there is a role reversal, and the parent becomes the emotional burden of the child. Not only does this never fix a parent, but also it always breaks a child. It stunts a child's emotional development as it robs him or her of a normal childhood.

Parents, your children need you, but you should not need your children in the same manner. If you have unmet needs, hurts, insecurities, or other issues, turn to God and healthy adult relationships to get those needs met. Don't use your children to prop yourself up.

Check yourself with these guidelines:

- Are you able to discipline your children properly and enforce parameters without fear of harming or losing your relationship with them?

- Are you so absorbed in your children's lives that you do not have time for other interests or relationships?

- Are your children the first place you turn with hurts and emotional needs? (The only time this is appropriate is if your children are adults. Even then, you need healthy relationships apart from them. If you're married, your best friend and confidant should be your spouse. Remember, even your grown children need space to develop their marriages and lives apart from you. Codependent parenting when your children are young sets you up to be a problem in-law when they are grown.)

If you realize that you or your spouse is codependent, address the issue seriously. If you cannot resolve it, get help. You cannot afford to allow an unhealthy dependence of any sort to divide you, because it will only exaggerate and perpetuate the problem.

The solution is for husbands and wives to turn to God individually, and then together to meet their needs through a daily personal relationship. Communicate. Don't be separated and turn elsewhere for help. Work at understanding each other and supporting one another. Stand as a united front to love and discipline your children. That's what they need, and it is what will make you the healthy adults you need to be to provide the foundation for a functional, healthy home.

(There is more information to help you understand the importance of healthy dependence and how it affects your family in my book, *7 Secrets of Successful Families*.)

The Great Parental Divide

In Luke 11:17, Jesus gives us that great nugget of truth: *"A house divided against itself falls"* (New American Standard).

Nowhere is this as true as in the area of parenting. When parents are divided, the enemy can play at will. He loves division. In fact, division is the devil's specialty. He constantly works to divide homes, churches, nations—any place where there are two people. For no one understands better than he the power of unity.

Jesus said, *"Again I say to you that if two of you agree on earth concerning anything that they ask, it will be done for them by My Father in heaven. For where two or three are gathered together in My name, I am there in the midst of them"* (Matthew 18:19-20).

Jesus promises powerful results if just two people will agree. He also promises His intimate presence when two people are gathered in His Name—and to be gathered in His Name means we are together to accomplish His purposes.

When parents come together to accomplish God's purpose in their children's lives and they are in agreement—they are unstoppable. Satan fears this kind of unity among parents and works feverishly to foster division.

Now, parents, that doesn't mean you have to believe all the same things in exactly the same way to be in *unity*. You only have to agree on the important matters. Nonetheless, never allow your children to see you divided as parents. If you hit a point where you both disagree, do it privately and come into agreement for their sake.

The most important issue that is necessary for parents to agree on is submission to God. If two people are submitted to God and their first consideration is His will, it won't be hard to find agreement. After all, true submission means being humble—and two humble people can easily find common ground.

Furthermore, true submission to God means recognizing His Word as the highest authority of life—and God's Word is quite clear when it comes to the issues of life, including parenting.

United parenting means you take time to communicate, pray and agree about those things that affect your children. Sacrifice to understand each other and make any necessary compromises – realizing that unity is more important than accuracy in most situations.

In contrast, agreement is much more difficult for people who are selfish and stubborn. Even then, parents who care for their children must realize how damaging and stressful it is for their children to grow up in a home where their parents are divided.

One of the most important things a child needs is security. Children are very sensitive to the emotional state of their parents and their marriage. When parents are divided and argue, it causes insecurity and anxiety for children.

Also, when parents are divided, children intuitively know how to take advantage of it to get what they want. They will quickly discern the weaker or more permissive parent on any issue and manipulate that parent to get their way.

Again, this damages the marriage because there is resentment that is created by one parent dishonoring the wishes of the other. It also damages the children because they are being raised in a home with divided parents. Not only will they grow up with emotional problems, but later in their own marriages they will be at a disadvantage in understanding the proper way to parent their children and relate to their spouses.

Parents, work hard behind closed doors to find agreement on every significant issue on your parenting. Then decide how it will be communicated to your children. I cannot stress how important it is that both of you act as a united front to your children.

Remember, the key word in parenting is *we*.

"*We* want you in bed by 9 o'clock...."

"*We* want your room cleaned up before you go outside...."

Also, honor each other in front of the children, Mom and Dad. Dishonoring your spouse in front of your children means you are divided.

And don't allow dishonor of the other. Allowing your children to dishonor your spouse while you sit idly by is divided parenting, as well.

United parenting means you take time to communicate, pray and agree about those things that affect your children. Sacrifice to understand each other and make any necessary compromises—realizing that *unity* is more important than *accuracy* in most situations. In short, united parenting is one symphonic voice of love and truth in the ears of your children.

Yes, parenting is a challenge. But it is one easily mastered by a husband and wife working as partners and using their committed relationship as the platform of positive parenting.

Chapter Eight

Resolving the Stress of
Parent and In-Law
Problems

In-laws. Every marriage has them. They are often the brunt of jokes. Oftentimes, however, those jokes are not too far from the truth.

Nonetheless, in-laws can be a great blessing to any marriage—but only if they are respectful of the parameters of their children's marriage and the sovereignty of their family unit. The real in-law problems come when there are either no clear parameters to the parent-child relationships, or the existing parameters are violated.

First Things First: Leaving, Then Cleaving

The very first thing God's Word says about marriage is, *"For this cause a man shall leave his father and mother..."* (Genesis 2:24, New American Standard).

Before a man and woman can do any "cleaving" in marriage, there has to be some "leaving." And that goes for both of them. For if either spouse is unwilling to reprioritize parents as less important than a husband or wife—in real terms—it will damage, if not destroy, their marriage.

In almost every case where I have counseled couples fighting over in-law problems, the resentment was much more focused on the spouse whose parents were intruding than on the in-laws, themselves.

It doesn't take much to figure out that in-laws cannot violate a marriage without the help of a spouse. Consequently, if a problem with in-laws is not dealt with decisively, it can ruin the intimacy and trust of a marriage.

Many in-law problems end in a couple divorcing, because there is stress caused by the knowledge that someone outside the marriage is controlling it, and will most likely continue to do so.

According to God's plan, when a couple gets married, they are to become a sovereign and sacred union under Him. Control of the marriage by anyone outside of it is against God's design, and it damages the integrity of the relationship.

Sometimes, however, couples unknowingly invite control into their marriage by including parents in the process of their making decisions or addressing certain issues. Many of them say, "Oh, but we have a very close family."

In reality, what they're calling "closeness" is actually a violation of their marriage's boundary, and in most cases, the spouse whose in-laws cross that line will be the one to resent it. Even if he or she does not object, it is unhealthy for a couple to not have the proper amount of time alone, and to decide important issues between themselves.

One couple I knew spent almost every night, nearly every weekend and most vacations with the wife's parents. This went on for years. They all practically lived together, and no one seemed to mind. The facade remained intact until one day the husband had an affair. Eventually, they divorced.

Certainly, the husband's behavior could not be blamed on his wife, or his in-laws. Yet, it could be explained by a lack of emotional bonding in their marriage. They were not away from the in-laws long enough to be able to focus on each other, build intimacy and meet each other's needs.

In the end, what the couple touted as a close relationship with the wife's parents was actually an emotional prop to hide the faulty foundations of their weak marriage. They violated God's design, and they paid the ultimate price for doing so.

When in Doubt...Honor

Karen and I are blessed with great parents who are also great in-laws. We have a close relationship with both sets of parents, without any negative issues. Being in-laws, ourselves, we relate to our children and their spouses in the same spirit as we do our parents—we are close with them and see them regularly, but we respect their need for "space."

Personally, I believe in the old saying, "Good fences make good neighbors." The point is simply that relationships succeed when there are clear, fair boundaries.

To help you understand what are appropriate boundaries concerning in-laws, and how to establish them in your marriage, there are four principles I want us to examine. I believe these principles will help you have the best possible relationship with your in-laws.

The first principle is *honor*.

From the very beginning, God instructed us to honor our fathers and mothers (Exodus 20:12). Honoring our parents means we are to respect them privately and publicly, whether they are perfect or not. It also means we are to be careful about the attitudes we hold toward them.

Though we are told as adults to honor our parents, we are under no obligation to obey them. They hold no authority over us when we are grown. Children are the ones commanded to obey their parents (Ephesians 6:1).

Yet, many children grow up, leave home, get married, but never realize their parents' authority over them is no longer present.

To further complicate matters, adult children can often have a difficult time refusing their parents' desires or directives due to their desire to please their parents, just as they did when they were growing up.

Whatever the case may be, the truth still stands that any time parents control an adult child, it harms the child's marriage and demoralizes the child's spouse.

As adult children, then, we must be willing to refuse *respectfully* the control of our parents. Still, if it comes down to parents trying to use money, shame, guilt, threats, or any other means to try to control us, our spouses or our children, we must stand up to them.

The challenge to standing up to our parents is to do it with love and respect. Certainly, it may be unpleasant, but it will cause them to respect us. More importantly, it will protect our marriage. Standing up to a parent can be one of the most difficult things we do in life, but we must do it when necessary. If we don't do it, no one will.

Refusing a parent's control is usually a defining moment that marks passage into adulthood. It means you have come to recognize who you are and your ability to stand on your own. If you lack a willingness to make that stand, it means you have not developed your wings, or you don't have the confidence to fly without your parents' permission.

Keep in mind, though, the longer you allow your parents to control you, the longer you will be robbed of the joys of maturity and spreading your wings. And if you are married during that time, your parents' control over you will not only ground you, but also it will ground your marriage.

Now, if you or your spouse are in a situation where you work for your parents or in-laws, understand that their authority over you is only limited to your employment. If they try to expand their authority beyond the boundaries of employment into your personal life, you need to lovingly confront them. If that doesn't work, don't be employed by them.

Another situation to approach with caution is when your parents or in-laws give you money. On one hand, that can be a blessing. On the other, it can often become a means of controlling you, your marriage or your children.

Certainly, an exception would be if you went to your parents for financial help. If they're giving you money to bail you out of a problem, it's not wrong for them to state certain conditions or desires to protect their investment. But those conditions still need to be within reason.

Regardless of any conditions, however, your parents' or in-laws' help does not *buy* them a permanent seat on the board of directors of your life. They're never allowed a "controlling" interest.

The bottom line is, honor your parents and your in-laws—no matter what they do. Honor them to their faces. Honor them behind their backs. Honor them when life with them is wonderful. Honor them when life with them gets frustrating. If you honor them in that way, Exodus 20:12 promises you a long life and blessing.

You Have to Leave to Cleave

As I said earlier, the first thing God ever said about marriage is that we have to leave our mothers and fathers in order to cleave unto our spouses. *Leaving* simply means making that healthy separation between you and your parents for the sake of bonding with your spouse.

When there is a problem with leaving, most often it's a matter of a parent who won't let go of the child. Usually it's mothers, more so than fathers, who have a hard time letting go. That's why for generations mothers-in-law have been stereotyped as being intrusive and problematic for their children's marriages. But, certainly, that's not always the case.

Still, the most difficult of relationships is usually between a wife and her mother-in-law.

Typically, the mother-in-law is insecure and jealous of her daughter-in-law. Suddenly, the son who once depended upon her is now depending on another woman.

It is so important that a son not allow his mother to criticize or undermine his wife—her cooking, her abilities as a wife and a mother—or his relationship with her.

By the same token, it's important that a son not complain about his wife to his parents.

A rule of thumb is, if you and your spouse need any kind of advice or marriage counseling, go to a pastor, a godly friend or Christian counselor. Don't go to your parents.

Now, the other side to this "leaving" issue is that parents need their space, too. They need church, friends, hobbies, as well as time for their own marriage. Even if you have a parent who is widowed, he or she still needs interests and relationships apart from you.

Couples sometimes allow a parent or in-law to intrude into their marriage because they feel sorry for him or her.

For example, you may have a parent who sits at home alone and lets everyone know how lonely he or she is and how much a visit from you would mean. Well, studies have shown that even parents whose children are close to them get lonely if they don't have friends their own age. Responding to feelings of guilt or sorrow about your parent's loneliness will not fix your parent, but it will break you.

If you have parents like this, encourage them to get involved in church, outside interests or volunteer work. The point is to build other relationships. If they refuse, don't feel sorry for them and don't sacrifice your marriage to make up for their stubbornness. Just let them know that you love them and will spend an appropriate amount of time with them.

In general, problem in-laws usually fit a profile. To begin with, they're usually widowed, or have a weak relationship with their spouse. They often lack significance in other areas of life. They're usually overly attached to their children and derive too much of their self-worth from them. Consequently, they have a difficult time letting go when their kids leave home. And they typically become adversarial with their children's spouses.

If you see a parent lining up with this profile, take the responsibility to pray for them, to love them and to tell them the truth. And the truth is, you're not responsible for "fixing" them. It may break your heart to confront these kinds of issues, but better that than allowing it to break your marriage.

Now, if you have parents going through severe times, such as a serious illness, you should always be committed to caring for them. That would include giving grace to your spouse if he or she is having to tend to a parent, or parents. But if you are the one having to attend to a parent, be careful not to ignore the needs of your spouse for too long, or too frequently.

Also, if you're in a situation where a parent needs to live with you for a while so you can care for him or her, know that this is rarely a wise long-term solution. You should probably consider other options.

The principle of separation is important, but it doesn't mean that we shouldn't care for our parents in times of genuine distress and need. In fact, the way we care for our parents and honor them as they age and go through difficult times should set a good example to our children.

Finally, on the more proactive side to all this, you can ensure you have enough time *alone* with your spouse—and your immediate family, if you have children—by setting boundaries for your relationship with your parents and in-laws. Those boundaries can be as simple as asking them to call before they come over to your house for a visit. Take the initiative to place limits on the frequency of your parents' visits, and the length of their visits.

As you take these practical steps and follow them consistently, your marriage will have the separation—or *leaving*—necessary for you and your spouse to be able to *cleave*.

The Enforcer

The next principle to remember when establishing boundaries in your marriage when it comes to parents and in-laws is *protection*.

This principle of protection follows closely on the heels of *separation*, or leaving, because it's basically just enforcing the boundaries you've established by separating your household from that of your parents and in-laws.

You are responsible for protecting your marriage and family from the intrusion of your parents. While it can be very difficult and awkward for you to tell your in-laws to "back off," it is by far much easier for you to communicate this kind of "tough love" to your own parents.

Though Karen and I have been married nearly 30 years, I am still highly cautious of correcting Karen's parents. Karen, however, can easily do it because of her relationship with them. The same is true of my parents. It's much easier for me to confront my parents when it comes to reinforcing boundaries than it is for Karen.

Like it or not, you are the one responsible for communicating and enforcing the parameters of your marriage to your parents, particularly when problems arise concerning those parameters. If you don't take on that responsibility, you are setting up your spouse to become an open target for your parents to criticize or to try and control. Even if your spouse refuses to tolerate any kind of control from your parents, there will still be damage to your marriage because you were not willing to stand up for your spouse.

Now, there are a couple of exceptions to this principle of protection.

The first is when one or both in-laws have an overpowering personality and you and your spouse agree that, of the two of you, the non-related spouse is the one strong enough to deal with them. In this case, the non-related spouse should be the one to address the issue at hand. But you must both still be in agreement and act as a united front.

The other exception is when you personally need to confront your in-laws concerning a serious violation of boundaries in your marriage, and your spouse is either absent, or is not willing to deal with the problem.

An example would be child abuse, or some other type of destructive behavior. In a situation like that, you simply cannot sit back and watch the destruction happen before your eyes for the sake of protocol. No, you must protect your family and children—first and foremost.

Understand that the principle of protection does not undo the principle of honor. You're still required to honor your parents and in-laws. But while honoring them, you still have the responsibility to enforce boundaries in your marriage, making sure that nothing that they do adversely affects your marriage, your spouse or your children.

Keep It Friendly

Finally, in establishing appropriate boundaries so you can have the best possible relationship with your in-laws, you need to apply the principle of *friendship*.

I met a couple in my office one day who was having a problem with the husband's intrusive and controlling parents. It seemed that every time his parents came over for a visit, it wasn't long before they would take over the home and the children. They would even go to the extreme of rearranging furniture in this couple's house, taking over the disciplining of their children and criticizing the domestic skills of their son's wife. It was obvious the husband's parents felt as though they had an inherent right to run the home as long as they were there, and their extremely controlling behavior left the couple perplexed.

When the couple in my office asked me what they should do, I responded with a question.

"How would you respond if one of your friends came into your home and did what your parents are doing?" I asked.

"We wouldn't tolerate it!" they quickly replied in unison.

"Then what's so different about your parents that you would allow them to get away with it?" I fired back at them.

They both looked at me with that *I've seen the light!* look.

The couple immediately knew that it would be inappropriate for a friend to act as these parents were acting. Yet, they realized that they had been tricked into applying a different set of rules for his parents...just because they were *family*. In this case, there is no different set of rules.

Granted, when you marry, your parents are still more important than your friends. Your relationship with them is very precious. Nonetheless, when it comes to your home and the boundaries within your marriage, no one has the right to walk in and take over.

When Karen and I go to our children's homes, we respect them and act toward them the same as we would if we were at a friend's house. We don't try to take control. We don't show up to criticize. We don't do anything differently, or behave any differently, than we would if we were visiting a good friend.

Love your parents as the dear family they are. But when it comes to what you do and do not allow them to do to you or around you—remember the principle of *friendship*.

Certainly, we all owe a great deal to our parents for their love and sacrifice in raising us. But as we remember all of the good they've done for us in the past, and as we honor them for their valuable presence in our lives, we must do so with a good *fence* between us.

The fence should not be so tall that we cannot see them, or so wide that we push them too far away. Yet, that fence must be tall enough and wide enough to make sure it cannot be stepped over or ignored.

Hence, the only way across the fence is to walk through a clearly marked gate that we have opened *together* for them as we both guard it vigilantly from being violated.

Chapter Nine

Resolving the Stress of
Communication Problems and Unmet Needs

Men and women are vastly different in the way God has designed them. If we understand those differences and respect them, they become a dynamic part of our marriages and are the spice of our lives together. If we don't understand them, they are dangerous and become a source of never-ending frustration and painful rejection.

That's why, in this chapter, I want to focus on the God-designed differences between you and your spouse, as well as how to honor those differences. The more you understand your differences, the more it can explain all those conflicts and tensions you've had in the past.

More importantly, understanding how you and your spouse are different will help you communicate better in your spouse's "language" and empower you to meet his or her needs.

When Boy Meets Girl

In all the marriage counseling I've experienced over the years, I can say with confidence that the fundamental differences between a man and a woman are the source of most marital problems. I can also say that each couple's response to those differences is what will either make or break their marriage.

The pattern I have seen over time goes something like this:

Boy meets girl. Girl meets boy. Boy likes girl. Girl likes boy.

Boy and girl fall madly in love. Boy and girl become consumed with each other.

Boy and girl get married. But boy and girl do not live happily ever after—because somewhere after the honeymoon and during the "settling down" part, boy and girl take that vast reservoir of energy they once used to *love* each other with, and they start using it to try to *change* each other.

For husbands and wives to succeed in communicating and meeting each other's needs in marriage they simply need to face the fact that they are different...and then take it from there.

The problem is, neither one of them understands the inherent differences they have as a man and woman, and before long they find themselves unable to communicate or meet each other's needs.

That's the point where the marriage starts heading downhill—and most marriages usually reach that point, at one time or another.

Karen and I hit that point in the first year of our marriage. We were both 19 years old, and I can honestly say that I was dumber than a tree stump when it came to women and marriage.

I had grown up in a home with four men and one woman. And I didn't have a clue about the unique nature of women and their needs.

So, when Karen came into my life, I watched her and listened to her, and

Communication Problems and Unmet Needs

I genuinely thought she was weird. As she tried to communicate with me and express her needs, I simply could not comprehend it.

Finally, I decided that God must have put me in Karen's life to help straighten her out, so I enrolled her in the "Jimmy Evans' School of Women Training." She dropped out.

To make matters worse, because I had told Karen on many occasions that I thought she was "officially strange," she became emotionally scarred and gradually withdrew from me.

Who wouldn't?

Obviously, what I didn't realize about Karen at that point in my life was that she was really quite normal—for a woman. I just didn't realize women were so different from men.

From Karen's perspective, she too had a hard time understanding my needs and unique nature as a man—and understandably so, because she was far more *relational* than I was.

Consequently, she also made the mistake of trying to change me into *her* image.

I remember that when I would approach Karen and tell her of a need or desire that I had, she would often roll her eyes or make a sarcastic comment about it. Every time she did that, I felt frustrated and rejected by her.

Needless to say, the result of our being ignorant about our differences was a complete communication breakdown. We fought constantly and with greater intensity as time went on. Both of us started accumulating unmet needs, as well as plenty of rejection. We were headed for disaster.

Admit It...You're Different

To succeed in communicating and meeting each other's needs in marriage, you simply need to face the fact that you are *different*...and then take it from there.

Once you get it straight in your head that your spouse is different from you – and he or she is supposed to be because God made him or her that way – then you can begin to work toward embracing those differences, instead of rejecting them. And that's important, because to reject your spouse's differences is to reject him or her.

If you married someone who is "normal," then I guarantee you that your spouse is as different as night and day from you.

As I said earlier, don't buy the lies our society propagates through much of the entertainment industry, through pornography, soap operas, romance novels, and just outright wrong information.

Those cultural influences promote the deception that "there's someone out there" who has the body of the opposite sex, but the exact same temperament as you. That's simply not true.

Once you get it straight in your head that your spouse is different from you—and he or she is supposed to be because God made him or her that way—then you can begin to work toward embracing those differences, instead of rejecting them. And that's important, because to reject your spouse's differences is to reject him or her.

Think about it. You finally reach the point where you're willing to risk being vulnerable, so you open your heart up to your spouse and begin to share some deep thoughts or desires...and then your spouse rejects or mocks you.

That kind of rejection from your spouse is devastating. And if it happens for long, you will eventually close yourself off from your spouse.

Rejecting one another over this issue of differences is the primary reason couples end up not being able to communicate and meet each other's needs.

More often than not, I find that it all comes down to a language barrier—men taking what their wives say and translating it into a language based on their own needs, and women taking what their husbands say and translating it into a language based on their own needs.

A good example of this is when couples try to communicate about sex vs. affection.

Sex is one of the primary needs of a man, but not so with a woman. High on a woman's primary needs list is non-sexual affection. That's why she often tells her husband, "I just want you to hold me." By that she means that she doesn't want it to be a prelude to sex.

Too often, though, when a woman approaches her husband for affection, he tends to reject her request as invalid because he doesn't have the same need. In doing so, he's actually using *his* needs as the standard for judging *her* needs. And with his needs as the "standard" for affection in their marriage, her needs are likely to never measure up. Therefore, the husband judges the wife's needs as invalid, and he rejects them—and her.

Another tendency in a man is to hear his wife's request for affection and misinterpret it as a come-on for sex. His brain says, *That is strange. Why does she want me to hold her? Oh, I get it—she wants sex!* So, rather than being affectionate, he becomes sexual and she gets frustrated. She clearly stated her need, but he translated it into his language...and it came out *sex*.

Now, understand that I'm not picking on the men, here. Women can also have some wrong tendencies when it comes to understanding their husband's needs.

Again, using sex as an example, most men have a greater need for sex than their wives do, especially men under the age of 45.

When a husband communicates his sexual needs to his wife, the woman will often reject his needs because his needs are usually so much stronger and more frequent than hers. I've counseled many couples where the wife so much as called her husband a "pervert" because he wanted sex so often.

So, as we saw with the man, this is a case of the wife using *her* needs as the standard to judge her husband's needs, and again, it only leads to deep resentment and frustration.

Likewise, the wife can also fall into the tendency of misinterpreting her husband's needs, just as we saw him do.

When a husband expresses his need for sex to his wife, she can often think, *You know, he says he wants sex...but what he really needs is to talk and be close to me. He just wants sex because he's not in touch with his true feelings. I can help him by refusing to give him so much sex and by training him to enjoy being more affectionate and romantic.*

Of course, that flow of reasoning will be just as big a flop for the ladies as it was for the men.

A great marriage exists only when both the husband and wife have their needs met. And their needs cannot be met until they are both willing to accept the validity of what the other is expressing, and they are committed to meeting each other's differing needs in a selfless, assertive manner. In order to do that, they first have to learn each other's language.

Closing the Door to Adultery...and Divorce

It is vitally important that husbands and wives get past the hurdles of any language barriers that might exist in their marriage. If they don't, their "unmet-needs" pile will start stacking up and will dramatically increase the likelihood of their having an affair or getting a divorce, or both.

An unpleasant statistic to report—but one that must be faced—is that about half of all men and a third of all women commit adultery or have an affair at some point in their married lives.

The truth is, nothing ever justifies adultery. It's always wrong and it's always devastating. Yet, the primary reason most people are drawn to commit adultery is because something is missing at home. While that certainly doesn't justify adultery, it does show us how we can minimize the risk of it. When we are not meeting our spouses' needs, it creates an inner hunger in them and in ourselves that is dangerous.

Remember, we have an enemy—the devil—whose specialty is destroying marriages. Unmet needs are his primary weapon in souring us toward our spouses...and sweetening the pot somewhere else. The Apostle Paul warns of this potential problem in 1 Corinthians 7:3-5:

> Let the husband render to his wife the affection due her, and likewise also the wife to her husband. The wife does not have authority over her own body, but the husband does. And likewise the husband does not have authority over his own body, but the wife does. Do not deprive one another except with consent for a time, that you may give yourselves to fasting and prayer; and come together again so that Satan does not tempt you because of your lack of self-control.

> **Adultery is never a solution, even though your needs may not be getting met by your spouse. The answer is to make the necessary deposits in your marriage. Be sure you are investing into each other, listening to each other and meeting each other's needs. That's the only way to "affair-proof" your marriage.**

Paul was a realist. He knew the schemes of Satan well and realized that unmet needs in a marriage could open the door for heightened temptations and lowered resistance. Therefore, he directed husbands and wives to be attentive in meeting each other's needs.

Not only does this minimize the risk of attraction outside of the marriage, but it is also the key to a satisfying and intimate relationship.

In the popular book, *His Needs, Her Needs*, author Willard Harley explains a concept that he calls the "Love Bank." In teaching us how to make our marriages affair-proof, Harley uses the analogy of a "Love Bank" to explain how, every time you meet your spouse's needs, you invest in him or her. You make a deposit into their Love Bank. The more deposits you make, the healthier the Love Bank balance, which fuels the marriage relationship.

Harley points out that many times, after a couple has been married for a while, they stop investing as much in each other. When that happens, their Love Bank balances can become dangerously low. And that's what can lead the husband and wife to venture outside their marriage, looking for other investors.

The primary reason men have affairs is they find a woman who honors them and who is sexually open toward them.

The primary reason women have affairs is they find a man who will talk to them and who makes them feel special and valued.

Adultery is never a solution, even though your needs may not be getting met by your spouse. The answer is to make the necessary deposits in your marriage. Be sure you are investing into each other, listening to each other and meeting each other's needs. That's the only way to "affair-proof" your marriage.

Meeting each other's needs also closes the door on divorce. Because, like adultery, the chances of divorce dramatically increase where there are communication problems and unmet needs. I can tell you from years of counseling experience that trying to convince people to stay in a marriage where none of their needs are getting met is a difficult task.

But I Have Needs

To help you make the best deposits into marriage, I want to conclude this chapter by listing the four major needs of women and the four major needs of men. Understanding these primary needs will not only help you better communicate with your spouse, but it will also help you make those important high-yield investments into your spouse's Love Bank—the way your spouse needs you to do it.

A Woman Needs...

Security

At the top of a woman's list of primary needs, I place her *deep* need to know that she will be cared for in a sensitive and sacrificial manner. She needs *security*.

A woman's need for security permeates every area of her life. Nothing makes her feel more secure than a selfless, sacrificial man. And, certainly, nothing makes her feel more *insecure* than a selfish, distracted man.

In Ephesians 5, the Apostle Paul commands husbands to love their wives just as Christ loved the church—by sacrificing their lives for her. He exhorts men to "nourish and cherish" their wives as they would their own bodies.

The secret to a woman's heart is to make her feel desired and valuable.

The secret to a woman's heart is to make her feel desired and valuable. So, if you want to succeed, gentlemen, you must be committed to bringing your wife to her highest potential by sacrificially and faithfully meeting her needs. That's what Paul means by the terms "nourish and cherish." Those are agricultural terms that speak of bringing something to "full maturity and fruitfulness."

When a woman knows her husband's heart is turned toward her, and that he is her biggest fan, she will blossom to her fullest. But if she feels she's being used, ignored or abused, she will wilt.

Because women need an environment of provision and protection, they choose their mates much differently than men do. Though women look for outward attractiveness in a mate, they are not as geared toward "appearance" being a factor in their choice as men are. In fact, women are usually willing to sacrifice physical attraction to some extent in order to find a man who has the characteristics of a good provider, father and protector.

That's why it's so important for a husband to communicate to his wife how committed he is to meeting her needs.

By the same token, that's how a woman intuitively knows when her husband's heart is turned away from her and their home.

Men, let your wife know you're committed to her and the kids, and that she won't have to nag or beg you to get results out of you. Affirm your wholehearted love and care for her.

By the way, romance is critical to the security of a woman. To a woman, romance simply means her husband meets her spoken and unspoken needs—*on his own* (without having to be told)—in a regular, creative and self-initiated manner.

That, gentlemen, is one of the most powerful ways you can communicate to your wife that your heart is turned toward her and that you're thinking of her, even when you are apart.

Open, Honest Communication

Women don't want "headlines"—they want the "whole story." That's why a woman's need for communication is as profound as a man's need for sex.

Did you get that, men?

In fact, when a man openly communicates with his wife, it actually increases her level of sexual responsiveness.

Communication is a lifeline to a woman. It is literally the supply line from her husband's heart to her own. Consequently, her well-being in marriage is highly dependent upon a regular flow of positive and meaningful dialogue with her husband. If all she gets is silence, or criticism and verbal abuse, it will devastate her emotionally and cause her to shut down.

Soft, Non-Sexual Affection

Remember this one, men?

We discussed earlier how your wife needs to be touched and held in a tender way that is not intended to lead to sex. But you may be surprised to learn that—as with open, honest communication from you—your wife will actually become more sexually responsive to you the more soft, non-sexual affection you give her.

The reason is, affection makes a woman feel valuable and secure. Whereas, the lack of affection makes her feel unattractive and insecure.

Men, you need to discipline yourself to be affectionate in private, as well as in public, with your wife. Holding hands, hugging, putting an arm around her, non-sexual kissing, verbal affection—that's speaking in *her* language. Trust me, it speaks volumes.

I grew up in a family that never openly expressed affection. To make matters worse, I constantly fought with my older brothers. So, when Karen and I started dating, I didn't know how to show affection without being rough. When I held her hand, I would squeeze it too hard and she would pull away.

I actually thought the problem was that Karen was too tender, but that her hand would *toughen up* over time. (I told you I was dumb.)

The real problem was that I had no idea how to be affectionate in a tender way. And this carried over into our sex life after we married. I was always too rough, and it caused Karen to be rigid and constantly defensive.

Needless to say, I had to work hard at changing. With God's help, I was able to discipline myself to show Karen the soft, non-sexual affection she needed.

I can remember the first time I held Karen's hand without actually cutting off the blood flow to it—I felt like an Olympic gold medalist. She loved it, too.

I'll add this, too, men. The more affectionate I became toward Karen in gentle, non-sexual ways, the more it enabled me to be more demonstrative toward our children. So, it blessed Karen and our kids immeasurably.

Leadership

No woman wants to be dominated, but every woman wants her husband to be a loving leader. She especially needs him to lead and initiate in the following areas:

Money—to be a good provider and to initiate discussions and decisions for the family's short-term and long-term financial well-being.

Children—to pay attention to the children and make sure that issues related to discipline, friends, boundaries, education and spirituality are addressed in a timely manner.

Spirituality—to initiate times of prayer together and lead the family in church involvement and worship, while developing their own personal relationship with God, helping them to be moral and ethical.

Romance—to initiate special times together and activities that build their relationship—and doing it without having to be guided in every detail, or nagged; that includes giving her flowers, cards, gifts and regular expressions of love and affection.

A man is a leader in his wife's eyes when he's responsible, proactive and doesn't need her to *lead* him to get things done. As he leads, he treats her as an equal and values her input.

It's that kind of leadership, gentlemen, that will meet a very important need in your wife, as well as provide an atmosphere in which your children can grow, develop and reach their potential.

A Man Needs...

Honor

Don't let anyone fool you, ladies—especially not your husband—men's egos are just as sensitive and as vulnerable as you are physically.

That's why a man will always gravitate toward the place where he gets the most honor and has the greatest sense of significance—while moving away from the place where he feels insignificant and dishonored.

Honor and significance are the most profound, driving needs a man has.

That's why a man will always gravitate toward the place where he gets the most honor and has the greatest sense of significance – while moving away from the place where he feels insignificant and dishonored.

Man was created in the image of God, and Psalm 100 explains something interesting about God, which gives insight into men. It says that we only enter into His "gates" as we offer thanksgiving to Him, and we only enter into His "courts" as we offer praise to Him.

Sound like any man you know, ladies?

The "gates" and "courts" of a man's heart are never open to anyone he perceives to be critical, negative or threatening to his ego. That doesn't mean someone cannot say something that is negative or corrective. Yet, it does mean that the way someone approaches a man must be careful and considerate, or they will have no chance of getting past the gates of his heart.

Many a woman has sat in my office complaining that her husband would not "open up" to her. While I make no excuse for a selfish husband who refuses to open his heart to his wife, I cannot discount the many cases I've seen where the husband shut off his wife due to her dishonor toward him.

Ladies, understand that your husband is *extremely* sensitive to dishonor, criticism, sarcasm and lack of appreciation. I have found that what a woman many times will dismiss as an innocent comment to her husband was, in fact, a serious blow to his ego, just as if she had belted him in the stomach.

What's more, if a husband ever reaches the point where he complains to his wife about the way she talks to him, she will often blow it off with a comment such as, "Boy, don't you have an ego problem!"

Going back to Ephesians 5, Paul tells wives to honor their husbands just as they would Christ. That's not to put a wife down, or give her husband a license to dominate her. It is, in fact, the key to her husband's heart. The more she honors and appreciates him, the more he will open the "gates" of his heart to her and desire for her to be in his presence.

The standard Paul gives women in responding to their husbands is how they would treat Jesus.

How would you speak to Him?

How would you say something negative to Him, or share a frustration?

That's your rule of thumb, ladies, when it comes to relating to your husband.

Remember, your husband is very sensitive in this area. So, the way you say something to him is as important to him as what you are saying. If you damage or dishonor him in this area, admit it to him and ask him to forgive you. Also, let him know that you respect this need and will work hard to meet it.

Sex

As I've mentioned plenty of times already, sex is a very strong drive in men. And so as not to belabor what we've discussed at length earlier in the book, I would simply encourage you, ladies, to respect the fact that your husband's sexual nature and needs are very different than your own. Therefore, openly express to him that you understand this difference—that you accept it, and you are committed to meeting his needs.

Fun

Simply put, a man wants—*needs*—to have fun with his wife.

If you think about it, that's how couples fall in love in the first place. They call each other up, think of something fun to do, and then go do it. Most men I know would rather be with their wives than anyone else.

For instance, I have a friend who travels around the country playing golf with his wife. When he talks about her and golf, he beams. Their marriage is strong because they spend time together having fun.

Here's a warning you should take to heart, ladies: If you take fun out of a marriage, it becomes a business. And if you take the fun out of marriage, that means you have to go *somewhere else* to find it.

Though it's normal and healthy for husbands and wives to have friends and interests apart from each other—do not lose the *fun* in your relationship.

One of the most dangerous points in most marriages is when children come into it. Even though children are a blessing to you individually and as a couple, they can cause a woman to become distracted from her husband and absorbed in her role as a mother. This is even more common when a woman has children and works outside the home.

The danger during this phase of marriage increases when a man turns his heart away from his wife to find solace in work, sports, friends, church, and the like. To keep this from happening, you need to spend time together having fun, just as when you dated.

You know better than anyone what you and your spouse enjoy doing together. So, just do it! Make it happen. Don't let life become all work, or your marriage become a business partnership.

Sometimes, ladies, that means you must be willing to sacrifice to be with your husband. Furthermore, dress to be attractive to him. Take care of your health so you can be active and energetic.

In other words, just because you're married, don't stop pursuing him and trying to please him—just as when you dated.

The short of it is, it's an important need for a man to have his wife as his "buddy." Karen is my best friend. I'd rather be with her than anyone else.

Domestic Support

Women have a gift of turning a house into a home. And it is an important need in men for their wives to decorate, care for the home properly and coordinate meals.

That doesn't mean a man should be able to go home, plop down in a chair and his wife wait on him hand and foot.

No, men should bear an equal share of housework and responsibility with the children. It is wrong for men to put that burden on their wives and expect them to carry it all. It's even worse if the wife works outside the home and has to come home, work all evening and all weekend while her husband passively observes.

I help Karen around our house, and I don't make her pick up after me. We are "partners" in every sense of the word.

Nonetheless, Karen initiates the care of our home and planning of meals. Not only is she much better at it than I am, but it is her gift. That's because women are "nesters"—and they are amazing at what they do.

Consequently, releasing a woman's domestic instincts in a diligent manner meets a deep need in her husband as it creates an atmosphere that provides nourishment and rest for his body, mind, and soul.

* * *

I hope this chapter helps you to better understand your spouse—as well as yourself. It's a glimpse into God's wonderful design for you and your spouse, and His plan for your lives together in marriage.

Remember, understanding the important—and sometimes not so obvious—differences between you and your spouse will help you to expand the lines of communication between you, as well as enable you to meet each other's needs for the rest of your lives.

One final note: Though I only briefly discuss the four major needs of women and men in this chapter, my book and tape series, *Marriage on the Rock*, studies them in greater detail, while examining the whole issue of communication more thoroughly.

Chapter Ten

Resolving the Stress of
Abusive and
Destructive Behavior

Of all the problems that create stress and damage a marriage, living with an abusive or destructive mate is probably the worst. As a pastor and marriage counselor, I have seen many marriages destroyed because of the unrestrained passions of an unhealthy spouse.

Typically, it's the husband with the abusive behavior and the wife who is the victim. Amazingly, when I have counseled women who were victims of abusive husbands, they were often very confused about what they should do. Though they had endured great stress and pain, they still felt a desire to "work things out" if at all possible.

This "confusion" abused spouses struggle with—namely, *Do I leave...or, do I stick it out?*—is really the key issue that must be resolved in the *abused* spouse, before all the other issues in the *abusive* spouse can even begin to be addressed.

Abused Girls Become Abused Women

I have to admit that, when I first got into marriage counseling, I was fairly ignorant when it came to abusive and destructive relationships between husbands and wives. So, when abused women came to me, I primarily focused on helping them respond to their husbands. I was almost blind to the fact that, nearly every time I sat down to counsel one of these women, I was sitting across the desk from someone with little or no self-esteem, someone who was imprisoned to very warped reasoning.

The most perplexing thing was to see abused women passing through the doors of my office, going from one bad marriage to another...one abusive husband to another. Time after time I'd watch a woman who was "the salt of the earth" turn around and go right back to a man who was severely abusive or destructive.

After seeing enough of that craziness, I finally realized that, beneath the surface of most marriages in which there was abuse or destructive behavior happening over a significant length of time, there was a deeply rooted dynamic silently taking place between the abusive husband and his victimized wife. And it was a dynamic that a lot of these women didn't want to hear about.

The first step to healing that emotionally damaged girl and physically abused woman is for her to realize that she had problems long before she said, "I do."

The problem was, long before these women were being drawn into violent marriages, they had already been emotionally damaged. Usually, it was due to events in their childhood. Whatever the source, the bottom line was that they all felt unworthy of a "good" man.

So, what would they do as a result?

Go out and marry men who make them feel better about themselves. They might do so knowingly or unknowingly. Unfortunately, the men who usually met that criteria were men with a lot of problems themselves. That's when the woman would have to lie to herself and say, *Yeah...but I can change him.*

In other words, she was willing to play the part of savior as a trade-off to make her feel more secure in the relationship.

So, "emotionally-wounded" girl meets "messed-up guy." They marry...and somewhere down the road abuse and destruction begin.

One day, "emotionally-wounded" girl becomes "physically-abused" wife and asks, "God, why is this happening to me?"

Why Him?

The toughest—but most telling—question an abused wife can ask herself is, *Why did I marry him in the first place?*

Other important questions I usually ask abused women include...

- Did you marry your husband in spite of your better judgment?
- Did you see destructive tendencies in him, but you told yourself that you could fix them?
- Did his faults make you feel better about yourself?
- Do you avoid relationships with people who "have it all together"?

Their answers to these questions usually reveal the all-too-common pattern—and that's good. The first step to healing that emotionally damaged girl and physically abused woman is for her to realize that she had problems long before she said, "I do."

Now, if you are a victim in an abusive or destructive marriage, please understand that I'm not out to "expose" you, or make you feel uncomfortable. No, my sole purpose is to get you to deal with the root issues that are likely contributing to your marital problems and keeping them from being resolved.

Again, to stop the abuse or destruction in your home, you must be willing to accept the truth about yourself and deal with it. In doing so, you must also understand that abusive and destructive spouses need what I call an "enabler." They need someone who will actually help keep them on the track of wrong behavior.

The truest measure of love is whether you will do what is best for your spouse. And the best thing you can do for your spouse is to confront, and not allow him or her to get away with the abuse and destruction.

In other words, it takes two people to dance. An abusive spouse cannot be abusive unless his or her spouse puts up with it, and even facilitates it.

For instance, a victimized wife may act as though she's fed up with her abusive husband. But by never really dealing with her husband's problem decisively—by either just coping with it, running from it, or ignoring it—she is actually enabling her husband to continue in his abusive, destructive behavior.

Oh, there may be times when she attempts to stand up to her husband. Typically, however, he will manipulate or intimidate her into backing down from her threats.

Strangely enough, there may even be times when she—*the enabler*—blames herself for her husband's abuse or destruction. In doing so, she will then gloss over all the pain and problems she has endured as she recommits to her role as her spouse's savior.

In short, *the enabler* is trapped in a bad marriage, and will stay in that marriage until it crumbles around her. Then she will go out and start looking for the next "problem man" who needs a savior.

The truth is, this abusive husband could not get away with his behavior for long if he were married to a healthy, confident woman.

Now, that may sound harsh. But I've found that it often takes *harsh* reality to get couples to deal with destructive behavior honestly. They have a way of lying to themselves and blaming their troubles on other people.

Besides, if you're living with a truly abusive spouse, you're going to have to make some hard decisions at some point. The only way you can do that is if you are willing to face the facts about yourself, and allow the Lord to shine His loving light into the recesses of your soul.

The solution begins inside of you.

The truest measure of love is not expressed by your willingness to endure abuse, or remain loyal to a person who is destructive. The truest measure of love is whether you will do what is best for your spouse. And the best thing you can do for your spouse is to confront and not allow him or her to get away with the abuse and destruction.

Helping You Draw the Line

Up to this point, we have focused on the victims of abusive and destructive spouses. And for the sake of introducing the material, I spoke of abusive behavior and destructive behavior in general terms, combining the two.

Now, as we turn our focus on the spouses who actually inflict the abuse or destruction and the specifics of confronting their problems, we will separate the two behaviors.

First, we will address handling the abusive spouse.

In 1 Peter, we are told that Jesus suffered for us while we were still in our sins. Peter also tells us that we are to follow Jesus' example of suffering. God wants us to be willing to endure unwarranted suffering and hardship for others just as Jesus did for us. The purpose of that suffering is to redeem others through our righteous example and undeserved love just as Christ did for us. In that context, Peter wrote:

> Wives, likewise, be submissive to your own husbands, that even if some do not obey the word, they, without a word, may be won by the conduct of their wives, when they observe your chaste conduct accompanied by fear. Do not let your adornment be merely outward—arranging the hair, wearing gold, or putting on fine apparel—rather let it be the hidden person of the heart, with the incorruptible beauty of a gentle and quiet spirit, which is very precious in the sight of God.
>
> For in this manner, in former times, the holy women who trusted in God also adorned themselves, being submissive to their own husbands, as Sarah obeyed Abraham, calling him lord, whose daughters you are if you do good and are not afraid with any terror" (1 Peter 3:1-6).

Peter understood that women are more naturally relational and righteous than men. That doesn't mean men cannot be—just that women get there first.

Therefore, Peter calls on women to be the righteous redeemers of their husbands. He's calling on them to righteously suffer for their husbands because they are usually the ones who care most naturally about the spiritual and relational elements of life. So husbands need to see their example of undeserved love and righteous endurance in order to be inspired to change.

The loving example of a godly woman is a powerful force. Any woman can love a perfect man, but it takes a special woman to love a man who is imperfect and undeserving—which is why Peter directs wives to the high call of redeeming their disobedient husbands.

The truth is, every person is going to suffer in marriage. We are, after all, married to imperfect people who make mistakes. And when our spouses do something wrong, we suffer. It's a fact of life, something we all need to learn to deal with in a mature and righteous manner.

What I want to point out, however, is that there is a major difference between *abuse* and *suffering*. The difference is *damage*.

You can suffer and not be damaged. You suffer every day, but by God's grace you are still emotionally, physically, and mentally sound enough to go through life successfully. His grace gets you through it unharmed.

> **A woman can suffer through a tough marriage with a very imperfect husband and still remain healthy. In fact, when she turns her troubles to the Lord, a wife can even come out stronger than before. Not so with abuse. Abuse never improves a person. It only destroys.**

Abuse, on the other hand, damages people. Whether the abuse is physical, mental or emotional, an abused person is impaired. The longer the abuse continues, the more damage it does, and the more the person is negatively affected and handicapped by it.

In the beginning, the effects of abuse can sometimes be hidden or masked. But the damage is still there. As the abuse continues, it will manifest.

A woman can suffer through a tough marriage with a very imperfect husband and still remain healthy. In fact, when she turns her troubles to the Lord, a wife can even come out stronger than before.

Not so with abuse. Abuse never improves a person. It only destroys.

Now, I have found that, if you are in a relationship where you cannot decide whether you are suffering or being abused, you are probably suffering. Abuse is typically severe enough that an honest assessment will easily reveal the damage in yourself or your children.

If you are in a marriage in which you are suffering because of the errors or sins of your spouse, do as Peter directed. Trust in God as you righteously suffer for your husband or wife with a redemptive spirit. God will reward you for your faith and commitment to follow the example of Christ.

However, if you are in a marriage in which you or your children—or both—are being abused, you need to take the next step.

It Doesn't Just Go Away

Abuse gets worse when it is allowed to continue. That's why—at the first sign of it—you need to give a clear warning and follow through if your warning is violated. Abuse continues in a marriage when there is not a clear enough warning or strong enough penalty for it.

Let's say a husband gets angry and physically threatens his wife. The woman's unwavering response should be something like this: "I love you and I am committed to our marriage—but understand—if you ever strike me, or threaten me again, I will leave and not come back until you have proven you are different and will never do it again."

The real punch comes when, if he does become threatening or abusive just one more time, she packs her bags and leaves. She must stand by her words. If her husband genuinely wants her back, he will have to prove that he is willing to take responsibility for his actions.

Meanwhile, the woman needs to find a separate, safe place to live—with a family member, friends, or in a shelter for abused women.

Let me clarify that when I talk about *leaving*, I don't mean the woman should divorce her husband. I simply mean, she should find a place to live away from his abuse or threats. That means no cooking for him, cleaning for him, or meeting his sexual needs.

An abusive man has no motivation to change when he's able to abuse his wife and children, yet not lose anything. If it doesn't cost him dearly where it hurts, an abusive man has little chance of repentance.

There's nothing like the reality of an empty home and a lonely bed to give a man a wake-up call.

> **An abusive man has no motivation to change when he's able to abuse his wife and children, yet not lose anything. If it doesn't cost him dearly where it hurts, an abusive man has little chance of repentance.**

Once an abused wife does find a separate place to live, she can later express her love to her husband from a safe distance, while monitoring the fruit of his life. That's called a "constructive separation."

If, however, the husband abandons his wife because of her response to his abuse, or, if he doesn't take any steps to change over a reasonable period of time, it's the wife's choice to go on with her life. If that's the case, at least she reduced the damage to herself and her kids and gave her husband the best possible motivation to change. If an abusive man won't change when he knows it will cost him his marriage and family, it proves that he's not likely to ever change.

Abuse must be dealt with in a very serious manner. If not, the family will likely suffer long-term consequences. While everyone involved hopes things will change, they rarely do until the abuser is forced to accept responsibility for his behavior and get help.

Don't Be the Lone Ranger

One of the worst things abused spouses can try and do is to make all their decisions by themselves.

In the first place, they are hurting, and that is the worst time to make decisions.

Second, abusers are typically masters at manipulation and control. They can give you a black eye, and then convince you that it was *your* head traveling toward their fist too fast that caused the problem.

If you are the victim of abuse, do not allow yourself to become isolated or too embarrassed to get help. That's the very time you need to go to a pastor, an abuse center, or a Christian counselor. You need someone who will support you, someone with whom you feel comfortable, someone to whom you can go for advice and talk out your feelings.

In abusive situations, intervention is often helpful. *Intervention* simply means that a third person, outside of the marriage, steps in to stop the destructive behavior, support the victim and try to help the abuser. It's best if the person intervening has a relationship with the abusive spouse that will provide a platform of influence, but it's not necessary.

The most important goal, however, is for abused spouses to seek the support they need to be able to stand up to the abuse and stop the damage.

Also, if you are being physically abused or you feel threatened, notify the police immediately. Spousal abuse is a crime. Abusive spouses need to know that they cannot abuse someone without suffering the legal consequences. They need to know you have informed the police and will continue to do so anytime it happens again.

Don't feel guilty or try to prevent the full legal consequences from falling upon your spouse. Let your spouse suffer the penalty for his or her actions. It's not your fault. He or she must take responsibility for it.

Once you have sought the help of a third party and you have advised the police of the abuse, you should start thinking about long-term counseling and true accountability. Without it, it's likely that any short-term "cooling down" period between you and your abusive spouse will eventually degenerate...until you are back where you were before.

If an abusive spouse is genuine in his desire to change, he won't mind going to counseling or being held accountable. And that means getting help to deal with his anger and other issues.

In short, you need someone you can talk to, someone who can also keep your husband accountable anytime he displays negative behavior.

Finally, if you face outbursts of rage from an abusive spouse, remember that God works miracles in the lives of people who trust in Him. During times of suffering and difficulty, the devil always wants us to focus on the problem. The more we do, the bigger the problem seems and the more discouraged we become.

Certainly, it's important to take the practical, natural steps in confronting an abusive spouse. But this is also a time to focus on God. As you pray and turn your heart toward God, you will gain a different—a more positive—perspective. Your problems will seem smaller. God will seem bigger. What's more, by trusting God, you enable Him to change circumstances like nothing and no one else can.

On a spiritual plane, the only real solution for an abusive spouse is a genuine change from the heart. And God is the only person who has access to a person's soul. Only He can be with each person 24-hours-a-day, understanding what's going on—what's going wrong—and how to fix it.

So, if you are being abused, don't focus on the problem or try to carry the emotional burden of the situation by yourself. Trust God. Believe Him for great things. As you pray, be specific. In fact, keep a journal of your prayers, along with God's answers to them. It will encourage you and help build your faith during these trying times.

Also, get involved in a church where the Bible is preached, if you're not already. Families are blessed when they worship together regularly. Church fellowship and regular worship are essential elements in your ability to live successfully.

Being a part of a church like that will also help keep you supplied with godly friends, who can in turn keep you accountable, pray with you, encourage you and just "be there" when you need them.

Keep in mind that the lack of a sound spiritual structure in marriages and families is one reason that abusive behavior occurs. So, as you demand true change and accountability from your abusive spouse, you should insist on worshipping together regularly and becoming involved in a good church.

Living in an evil world as we do, we all need the encouragement, accountability, and ministry that are unique to the church environment.

Perhaps you've heard the old saying, "The family that prays together, stays together."

Well, it's true.

So, commit to strengthening the foundation of your family's spiritual life. Go to church together. Pray together. Read the Bible every day.

The Bible is God's Word specifically to you, for today. It will give you spiritual life and enlightenment. It will give you practical advice and answers to every problem. Better still, His Word never fails.

If you and your spouse will read the Word, believe it and obey it, then you will succeed in everything you do. It's an essential part of every stable and successful life. Get a translation of the Bible that's easy for you to understand, and start reading it every day.

The Dangers of Destructive Behavior

As I said earlier in this chapter, there is a difference between abusive behavior and destructive behavior. We just have not needed to make the distinctions until now.

The term *destructive behavior* refers to actions that are significantly harmful or dangerous to an individual, the family finances, the family, other people, and so on.

An example of destructive behavior is a gambling addiction that squanders the family's finances and puts at risk the well-being of the home. Alcoholism, drug addiction, addiction to pornography—these can put tremendous stress on a family and they are always destructive.

As was the case with an abusive spouse, an "enabler" helps keep the destructive spouse in business by making excuses for him, covering up for him and shielding him from the consequences of his behavior.

I know of one man whose addiction to pornography cost him $70,000 in credit card bills, as well as three failed marriages.

So, a *destructive* spouse needs to be dealt with in much the same way as you would an abusive one.

First, you must deal with a spouse's destructive behavior in a decisive and serious manner.

Second, every destructive spouse—or addict—must have someone to *enable* his or her behavior if it's going to be tolerated in the home.

As was the case with an abusive spouse, an "enabler" helps keep the *destructive* spouse in business by making excuses for him, covering up for him, and shielding him from the consequences of his behavior.

Again, if you're facing destructive behavior in your spouse, don't *enable* it—confront it. As you confront it, make sure your spouse knows that you will not tolerate or enable his behavior in any way.

Also, make it clear to your destructive spouse that, if he refuses to take responsibility for his behavior and get help, there will be consequences. Be clear—and firm—as you communicate with him about what those consequences will be.

Remember, you must follow through on your warnings, just as with the abusive spouse. Do not accept crocodile tears or empty promises. Insist that your spouse go for regular counseling and real accountability until the issue is genuinely resolved and the fruit of change is bountiful and obvious.

If your destructive spouse refuses to face his problems, however, there may be a time when you have to resort to constructive separation to protect yourself and to issue a wake-up call.

I don't advise constructive separation lightly, and it shouldn't be done just to get your spouse's attention or to get your way in an argument.

Separation is a serious step. It can damage a relationship permanently if done for the wrong reasons. Constructive separation is an alternative to divorce that gives a person a safe place for protection from abuse or destructive behavior as it motivates the spouse to change.

Of course, dealing with *destructive* behavior in a spouse also requires outside counsel and wisdom. You may need some temporary intervention to help you confront and deal with the seriousness of the situation.

Finally, never let yourself become isolated in a destructive environment where you are trying to make decisions in the middle of emotional pain and turmoil.

Seek an objective, third person's voice to guide you in times of trouble. And, certainly, seek spiritual nourishment to ensure you stay healthy and don't become damaged by your circumstances. Find a qualified person who loves God, and let them walk with you and give you counsel. This is a critical issue in overcoming any problem you face in life.

> **Abusive and destructive behavior ignores the damage that is done to others as it acts with selfish abandon. The answer is not to allow it passively, or to divorce it immediately. The answer is to deal with it decisively.**

The more you humble yourself and get the help you need, the more strength and wisdom you have to face your circumstances successfully.

When we get married, there's no denying that everything our spouse does affects us—and everything we do affects them. Therefore, we must be careful of our actions and respectful of how they affect our spouse and our family.

Abusive and destructive behavior ignores the damage that is done to others as it acts with selfish abandon. The answer is not to allow it passively, or to divorce it immediately.

The answer is to deal with it decisively.

As you stand up for yourself and refuse to be an *enabler* to abusive or destructive behavior, you are doing the right thing. Just follow through as you trust God and rely on righteous people to stand with you. That's the best way to deal with a bad situation, and it will give you the greatest opportunity to win the battle for your marriage and family.

Chapter Eleven

Resolving the Stress of
Remarriage and the Blended Family

With the high rate of divorce in our nation, it's no surprise that the number of people who remarry is also high. As you might expect, the number of "blended" families—spouses with children from a previous marriage coming together as one new family—has increased as well. In fact, today, *blended* families comprise about half of the families in our nation.

The challenge for these remarriages and blended families, however, is that they have a higher rate of divorce than first marriages, and face even more difficult issues. While these statistics offer little hope, I want you to know that you can succeed in a remarriage or blended family. I have counseled many remarried and blended family couples over the years, and I have seen many who were very happy and successful. Yet, in every case, they had to knuckle down and deal with their issues in a committed and correct manner.

The complexity of remarriage and blended family issues can leave even the most experienced counselors scratching their heads. As Christians, however, we can be assured that God always provides answers—if we will seek Him and do things His way.

So, if you have remarried, or you're in a situation where you have a blended family, I want to offer you some clear answers and direction so you can navigate the stresses and problems, and reach a place of peace in your marriage and home.

Getting Past the Past

Divorce is devastating. There's no denying it. People who have been through a divorce tell me it's worse than death. And while the emotional pain of divorce is much like death, it goes on even longer.

Then, of course, there are the children caught in the middle. They are affected, and often seriously.

When people encounter pain, they often don't deal with their feelings correctly. Eventually, those painful feelings will catch up with them. Take *forgiveness*, for example.

Forgiveness is the most important factor that determines a person's emotional health and ability to relate to people properly. Yet, the pain inflicted by an ex-spouse is probably the most challenging to forgive.

When people who are wounded and betrayed from a previous marriage remarry, they begin their new marriage with a lower level of trust and a higher level of expectation – and that is a dangerous combination.

Consequently, when people who are wounded and betrayed from a previous marriage remarry, they begin their new marriage with a lower level of trust and a higher level of expectation—and that is a dangerous combination.

What's more, probably long before they enter that second or third marriage, they've made some "inner vows"—or promises to themselves—and those "inner vows" are dangerous to one's spiritual and emotional health.

Bitterness and judgment against another person are almost always the root of an inner vow. People make inner vows to comfort themselves. They promise themselves that they will never experience the same painful problem again.

Some examples of their vows might be...

- *No one will ever hurt me like that again!*
- *I'll never let a man treat me like that again!*
- *I'll never let a woman treat me like that again!*
- *I'll never marry someone like that again!*

Though it's common for all of us to make comments like these at one time or another, they are wrong. To begin with, they demonstrate an attitude of not turning a situation over to God and allowing *Him* to lead us. Inner vows are self-directed promises. Here's what Jesus had to say about this self-directed attitude in Matthew 5:33-37:

> **Again you have heard that it was said to those of old, "You shall not swear falsely, but shall perform your oaths to the Lord." But I say to you, do not swear at all: neither by heaven, for it is God's throne; nor by the earth, for it is His footstool; nor by Jerusalem, for it is the city of the great King. Nor shall you swear by your head, because you cannot make one hair white or black. But let your "Yes" be "Yes," and your "No," "No." For whatever is more than these is from the evil one.**

Jesus warned against swearing things to ourselves, or anyone else. He even said that to do so is of the "evil one." That's a serious statement.

When we respond to situations in life by boldly swearing what we will and will not do, it makes us *God*. It's a form of arrogance and rebellion. And that's why it's wrong and of the devil.

Another danger of inner vows is they are always exacted from the people in our present and future. When you say to yourself, *No one's ever going to treat me like that again!* you are actually speaking about your future spouse. And, though your anger is at your ex-spouse, the price will be exacted from someone who is innocent.

> When you say to yourself, "No one's ever going to treat me like that again!" you are actually speaking about your future spouse. And, though your anger is at your ex-spouse, the price will be exacted from someone who is innocent.

Also, when the spouse comes along and does something to trigger your vow, your response will be much stronger and more volatile.

Unless you have forgiven your ex-spouse and those in your past who have significantly harmed you, you will carry the pain and problems into your future.

Do Yourself a Favor

The sometimes hard-to-face truth is, you must forgive and break all inner vows. Not only does God say you cannot be forgiven of your sins unless you forgive others, but the poison of unforgiveness inside you will damage you more than anyone else you can spew it on.

When you think about it, though, *forgiveness* truly is one of the most self-loving acts you can choose. Forgiveness means that you permanently erase the emotional and practical debt a person owes you, just as God does when He forgives you. Forgiveness also means you never try to punish others for their mistakes, in any way. You forget it. It's over.

Added to that, Jesus said you should bless the people who curse you, and pray for those who spitefully use you (Luke 6:27). That's the real key to healing and resolve.

As you begin to pray blessings on your ex-spouse and others in your past who have hurt you, it actually invites the Spirit of God to heal your emotions and to cut the cord from your past that is feeding your pain.

God is a forgiving God. He doesn't want to punish you for the rest of your life for the mistakes of your past. He just wants you to take responsibility for your behavior and turn your life over to Him. As you do, He will forgive you and give you the grace you need to succeed in life from that moment on.

Once you've forgiven and released all those people in your past, there's still one other person you need to face up to and forgive—yourself.

Perhaps you've made some mistakes in your past. Well, admit them before God and repent. And true repentance means you're committed to changing this area of your life and submitting it to God. If you realize you ran from the problems of your last marriage and that was wrong, then the test of your repentance will be that you don't run from the problems in your current marriage.

God is a forgiving God. He doesn't want to punish you for the rest of your life for the mistakes of your past. He just wants you to take responsibility for your behavior and turn your life over to Him. As you do, He will forgive you and give you the grace you need to succeed in life from that moment on.

Still, no matter how loving and gracious God may be, His forgiveness does not affect your life unless you are willing to *receive* it. Remember, you don't deserve grace. That's why it's grace. And it's free because you cannot afford it.

You will rarely *give* more grace to others than you are willing to receive from God, yourself. If you cannot receive God's forgiveness and grace for your mistakes, chances are, you will not be very forgiving and gracious toward the sins and problems of others. As the saying goes, "You cannot give what you do not have."

Purpose in your heart to receive God's grace to cover your mistakes and to empower you to live—today. The more of His grace you receive, the more it will flow out of you to encourage and bless others around you who are struggling.

Forgiveness is the key to being free from your past and ensuring a healthy future. If you have not forgiven your parents, a former business partner, your mate's ex-spouse, a friend, or anyone else, it will affect your overall disposition and your family relationships. You must forgive every day. That's why Jesus included the issue of forgiveness in the Lord's Prayer that we are to pray daily: *"Forgive us our trespasses, as we forgive those who trespass against us"* (Matthew 6:12, *King James Version*). These are the critical words that keep our hearts pure and enable us to love and be loved in a healthy manner.

Finally, be a good model and guide to your children in this area. They're struggling with unforgiveness, too. In fact, children can often feel deep anger and resentment toward a parent or stepparent. Many times, they will blame themselves and feel tremendous guilt for family problems. It's important that you help them realize that they are not at fault.

So, pray for—and with—your children, and help lead them to a healthy resolve of their emotions, too.

Starting Over Is Not the Same

Once you've addressed the issues of your past, you're now able to focus on the present—namely, your present marriage. And in *every* marriage, there are important decisions to be made that determine its success.

In remarrying, you will find many of those success-determining decisions to be the same. Yet, they are usually surrounded by much stronger emotions and fears that must be overcome. That's where I want us to examine three particularly vulnerable areas.

1. *Will you commit?*

As I said earlier, the danger of remarriage is that you can come into it with lower trust and higher expectations. Therefore, you must do everything possible to raise your level of trust and have realistic expectations. You must also avoid the "natural" tendency to wade in cautiously, rather than diving in completely. That's where dating comes into play.

The purpose of dating is to examine the character of another person and your level of compatibility. If you remarry "on the rebound," or without the proper dating process, you're likely to marry a person you are still sizing up. If you do not know whether this is the person to whom you want to commit, you will be set up for failure.

Regardless of the pain and mistakes of the past, plant your feet in the present. Commit to this marriage.

If you remarry "on the rebound," or without the proper dating process, you're likely to marry a person you are still sizing up. If you do not know whether this is the person to whom you want to commit, you will be set up for failure.

Without commitment, you will enter a vicious cycle of destructive behavior. Every time a problem exists, you'll wonder if it's what will break up your marriage. Because you think that way, you are not able to give *everything* to the relationship—and because *you* are cautious and uncommitted, your spouse will begin to withhold, as well.

In the end, your fears will come true. So, you will end that marriage and go on to the next. That's the very reason statistics say a person's chances of divorce rise every time he or she remarries.

You, however, can stop this from coming true in your life simply by making a firm decision to commit to your marriage.

Granted, there is no perfect marriage. *Every* relationship will have its problems. And even the best marriages are not without problems. Yet, they are the ones in which couples work through their problems together in a *committed* manner.

Author Linda Waite offers some fascinating research in her book, *A Case For Marriage*. In a study done in the late 1980's and mid 1990's, out of 5,232 married couples interviewed, 12.3% reported being unhappily married. However, five years later, of those who chose to stay together and work through their problems, 80% of them rated their marriages as "very happy."

Conclusion: Don't take a photograph of your problems today and tell yourself they will never change. That's exactly what the devil wants you to believe so you will give up and bail out.

Understand, however, if you totally commit and do the *right* thing, God will bless you and your marriage. But you must *commit* in order for your marriage to work.

2. Will you be "one"?

When God created marriage, He spoke these words as the constitution and guiding laws to make it successful: *"Therefore a man shall leave his father and mother and be joined to his wife, and they shall become one flesh"* (Genesis 2:24).

There are absolute laws that guide the institution of marriage. These laws are universal in that they affect every person, in all generations. Like the law of gravity, no matter who you are, if you violate it—you *will* suffer the consequences.

One of these marriage laws comes from the statement in Genesis 2:24—"the two shall become one." This is called the law of possession.

God designed marriage to operate as a complete joining and sharing of two lives. The intimacy and union of marriage is so profound that God used the word "one" to describe it.

And how do two things become one?

They meld.

In other words, in marriage, everything that was owned or administrated separately is now surrendered to the co-ownership and control of the relationship.

Consequently, anything you refuse to surrender to your spouse for his or her input and influence will damage your relationship and create deep resentment.

When it comes to remarriage and blended families, this matter of becoming one—or "control"— can get pretty touchy in two particular areas. The first deals with children from a previous marriage. The second relates to the consequences of the previous marriage or marriages.

If you have children from a previous marriage, you must *give* your children to your new spouse. You cannot withhold them. Likewise, if your spouse has children from a previous marriage, you must *receive* full ownership of those children.

Many parents who remarry try to treat their children as an exception to this rule. Because their children have been through a lot, the parents—especially mothers—will often try to protect them from further hurt. That usually means not allowing their new spouse to give input or influence regarding *her* kids.

If you think you're doing your children a favor by withholding them from your marriage to protect them, you're wrong. It only perpetuates insecurity within them as it allows them to divide you from your spouse and sabotage your new marriage. This is where you need to lose the word *my* and adopt the word *our*—whether it's with children, money or anything else.

Now, having said that, understand that you must remain sensitive to the emotions of the children and the particulars of your situation.

For example, it's usually better for a blended family if the biological parent *enforces* the discipline on his or her children. This is especially true when the marriage is new and the relationship between your children and your new spouse is still developing. But even then, your spouse must have input into the parameters of discipline and the overall disposition of the children. You must be a team and be influenced by each other.

I realize you may be thinking, *Yeah, but they're my kids and my spouse doesn't love them like I do.*

Thinking like that only perpetuates the fear that your spouse will not make the right decisions related to your children because he or she is not motivated by the same level of compassion and concern.

Certainly, your spouse may not love your children like you do. But let's face it—there's a biological bond in place that is one of the strongest forces in the universe.

Still, your spouse can love your children in a great way from a decision of the will, and not be as emotional about it as you are. In fact, the greatest form of love is *agape*. This is the love that Jesus demonstrated for us when He died for us on the cross. It's the only form of love that does not depend upon emotions. It chooses to love as an act of the will, not based on emotions.

3. *Will you embrace the good as well as the bad?*

Finally, when it comes to remarriage and blended families, the second area where life can get a little touchy is in dealing with the consequences of a previous marriage. By consequences, I mean child support, negative influence on the children by an ex-spouse, responsibility to care for biological or non-biological children during times of visitation, and so on.

One couple I knew divorced because the wife so resented the child support payment her husband had to make to his ex-wife every month. Instead of seeing the money as going to support *their* children, she saw it as being paid to *his* ex-wife. Every time the husband sat down to write the check, a fight would break out between them.

As with any marriage, husbands and wives who have remarried must understand that they're taking on all the good—and the bad—from each other's lives. You don't keep the *good* and throw out the *bad*. When you go through difficult times, you don't separate—you draw even closer.

Take on every difficulty as an opportunity to grow together as a team. That's the only way any marriage can succeed.

What's More Important?

Every family should be built around a marriage. A family built around children, or anything else, is like an atom without a nucleus. Without a nucleus, the atomic particles—the protons, neutrons and electrons—have nothing to orbit around.

In the same way, a family cannot be stable without a stable marriage at its core.

> **Every family should be built around a marriage. A family built around children, or anything else, is like an atom without a nucleus.**

In counseling, I often hear women say, "My children are permanent, but he (the new husband) may not be."

The problem with that kind of thinking is that the parent is giving more regard—more value or "weight"—to the children than the spouse in every decision. This is especially common in times of serious conflict.

The mindset is: *If this marriage doesn't last, I don't want my children to resent me for the rest of my life for choosing my spouse over them. So, I'll consider the possibility of divorce in this decision as I prefer my children over my spouse.*

A standard like that—controlled by fear—will only create a downward spiral of bad decisions, leading to bad feelings in the marriage, leading to the parent's fears coming true.

If you see yourself on this downward cycle, stop letting fear control you. Take control of your thoughts and let common sense and wisdom lead you.

Consider this:

- Your children are only in your home for about 18 years, but your marriage is for a lifetime.

- Your children cannot be equipped for success in their marriages and families if you don't provide a good example for them. They need to see you building a good marriage and working through your problems.
- The security and happiness of your children really depends on the stability of your marriage, so don't fear their response or let them control you. Just do the right thing and believe God for the right results.

If you truly want to succeed in your marriage, make your marriage your priority. Let your spouse and your children know through your actions, words and attitudes that you are committed to your marriage, and that it is your highest priority.

You can do that in ways that will not make your children feel rejected, or cause them to resent your spouse. Simply let everyone know that you are there to stay...and your marriage will not be laid on the altar of children's opinions, emotions or reactions.

Love the One You're With

We've covered a lot of ground in dealing with the foundational issues that need to be addressed in remarriages and blended families. But as we conclude this chapter, there are a handful of specific issues I will address, at least briefly.

The first is your feelings toward your ex-spouse.

I realize we've already discussed *forgiving* your ex-spouse. There is, however, another side to the coin for many people. I'm talking about feelings of love for an ex-spouse, feelings that may even be stronger than with their current spouse. Such feelings can haunt a remarried person and even sabotage their current marriage.

The reasoning goes like this: *This was a mistake...this marriage could never be as good as my first.*

Remember, the devil is evil. He will constantly accuse your spouse, and constantly try to divide you. He starts in with..."Remember the good times you had with your 'ex'? Weren't they great?" He's talking about the same person he convinced you was the scum of the earth a couple years ago.

Take control over those kinds of thoughts and feelings. Don't let them haunt you. It's just the devil doing his thing.

Besides, remember *agape*—the highest form of love? It's not based on emotion. It's based on a decision.

So, you decide. Don't let your emotions dictate your decisions. Let your decisions dictate your emotions. Don't keep looking over your shoulder and grieving. Do what one song suggests: "Love the one you're with." Focus on— and love—your spouse with your whole heart.

Where It Hurts Most

Perhaps the most heart-wrenching issue I see blended families deal with is the negative influence of an ex-spouse on the children and family. Oftentimes, the ex-spouse uses the children to exact revenge or cause pain.

In their book, *The Unexpected Legacy of Divorce*, Judith Wallerstein and Sandra Blakeslee make the astute observation that divorce is the only place where parents use children like bullets. I agree.

I have seen everything from the most bizarre displays of an unhealthy ex-spouse spoiling children, to indoctrinating the children against their other biological parent and their beliefs.

Here's what I tell parents facing that kind of craziness:

First, "This too shall pass." It will not last forever.

Maybe an ex-spouse is doing everything wrong that's possible. Just be thankful that you have time with the children to show them the right way.

Abraham Lincoln once said, "Let us have faith that right makes might."

The power of truth is greater than the power of lies. The power of love is greater than the power of hate. So, be confident, and keep doing the right thing—while believing God for the right results.

Also, be careful not to use your children to communicate with your ex-spouse for you. Do it yourself. Work hard to communicate and understand each other for the sake of your children. Sometimes a face-to-face meeting is best. But if it cannot be done in person, call or write a letter. Healthy lines of communication are important as the children go back and forth between households.

Now, in some cases, it may be easier for your new spouse to communicate with your ex-spouse on your behalf. But be wise. Make it clear upfront that the communication must be respectful, and that you and your new spouse are a united front and will not be divided by the "ex."

A critical point, for example, is that those times of communication are not for the ex-spouse and current spouse to share their common issues in dealing with you.

Also, make certain that any encounters you have with your ex-spouse are in a place where there would be no private or intimate contact between you. If you meet face-to-face, your spouse or another person should be present. This guards against any abuse or sexual temptation.

Finally, never speak evil of your ex-spouse in front of your children. Don't try to win your children to your side by making them bitter against your ex-spouse. Your children need to know that you have forgiven your ex-spouse, and that you wish the best for them, even if that's a real stretch for you.

Children are smart. They are not manipulated for long. They will eventually recognize what is going on. When they do, their respect will turn toward the parent who reveals the best character and the highest standards.

Remember, even though it may have been Grandma who gave you cookies all of the time, when you matured, you were more appreciative of your mother who made you eat your spinach.

So, don't be discouraged. Truth will prevail.

Raising the Standard of Propriety

One of the built-in protections God has placed in families is that we rarely view each other in a sexual way. Biological parents rarely view their children as sex objects, and biological siblings are rarely attracted to each other sexually.

This dynamic changes, however, in blended families. And the "natural" sexual protection is no longer present. That's why sexual abuse occurs more frequently between stepparents and their stepchildren, as well as between stepsiblings.

In blended family situations, this must be recognized, and certain standards need to be raised to ensure that problems are minimized.

First of all, there should be a higher standard for dress. Modesty must be maintained in a manner that is consistent with common sense and propriety. Immodesty leads to a higher level of sexual temptation.

Another important standard is that non-biological family members of the opposite sex should not spend time alone in an inappropriate manner. While it's virtually impossible to make sure that non-biological family members of the opposite sex are never left alone, that is not the point.

The point is that you do not allow it to become acceptable for a stepbrother and sister to be in each other's rooms with the doors closed. Do not allow it to become acceptable for a stepfather to tuck his teenage stepdaughter into bed every night for half an hour.

I'm not saying that the home of a blended family should be controlled by an attitude of suspicion or mistrust. I'm just saying it should be guided by common sense—realizing that there is a dynamic missing that is present in intact biological families.

Another important standard in blended families is that of listening to the children. Many times when children are being sexually abused, they will go to their biological parent and tell them something is wrong. This should not be dismissed. Sexual abuse by a stepparent or a stepsibling must be dealt with in a direct and serious manner.

Guess Who's Coming for Dinner?

Not only do almost all children want their parents who are divorced to get back together, but they normally view a stepparent as the end of their hopes of that happening. That's because children are intensely loyal to their biological parents, and they often have a difficult time adjusting to the remarriage of a parent and the presence of a stepparent.

The first thing that helps children to accept the reality of a new stepparent is to let them resolve their feelings about the past. Again, they need to forgive their parents, themselves, God, or anyone else they have not forgiven. And, if you've done something wrong concerning your child, you need to admit it and ask for their forgiveness.

Children also need to understand that the presence of a new boyfriend, girlfriend or spouse is not why you're not getting back together with your ex-spouse.

It is important that your children don't blame you for your failure to remarry their other parent. Spend time with them. Take them to receive professional Christian counseling if necessary.

A proper dating period is another way to help children adjust to a new relationship in your life—and theirs. That's why it's important that the *new* person is introduced into their lives one step at a time. Do everything you can to help them feel like they are a part of the process, and that it is not being forced on them.

Obviously, children will not make the final selection of your new mate, but they will play an important role in how your relationship with this new person will work. So, they need to be included in special times together that allow them to warm up to your new boyfriend or girlfriend, and learn to like them.

Preparing children properly for a new stepparent is an important process. It impacts their lives in a huge way, and they need careful guidance and consideration.

During this "warming up" period, it is important that potential stepparents do not immediately begin disciplining or correcting the children. Unless it is an emergency or very serious situation, the boyfriend or girlfriend needs to "earn the right" to correct the children. Even then, it must be done carefully.

What's more, boyfriends and girlfriends must also be careful to honor the ex-spouse—and not to try to replace or compete with them.

Even if a child is estranged from their other biological parent, or has negative feelings toward them, a potential stepparent must be careful not to take advantage of that or encourage it to continue.

The job of a stepparent is to be a good parent to a child to the degree that the child is in their care. They must promote and protect the health of the child's relationships with other family members—especially their biological parents.

Again, give it some time. Children do better over time. Do not get discouraged if they struggle for a while. After you marry, if you will be a united front with your new spouse to love and train the children, they will adjust.

In the beginning, the important thing is that your children know that you love them, and that their relationship with their stepfather or stepmother is allowed to develop naturally. While you must insist the children respect their new stepparent, avoid the mistake of trying to force them to go too far, too fast.

I'm sure there are many issues I have not addressed. Yet, I have at least covered some that will help you and address your needs to resolve the stress of a blended family.

Know that you *can* succeed if you remarry and blend your families. Indeed, there will be some special challenges. But there are also special rewards for those who dare to meet those challenges.

Chapter Twelve

Resolving the Stress of
Emotional Distraction, Emotional or Physical Abandonment, and Adultery

As I stated earlier, statistics tell us that about half the population of men, and a third of women, will have an affair at some point in their lives.

What those numbers don't tell us, however, is that there are many times when husbands and wives are not actually having an affair with another person, but they have emotionally abandoned ship or are emotionally distracted.

That's why many heartbroken wives have sat in my office and told me that they felt like their husband was having an affair with his job, or with a sport, or something else.

"At least if he were having an affair with another woman," they've confided, "I could compete. But how do I compete with this?"

To whatever degree someone leaves their marriage or violates their marriage covenant, the sad truth is, when a person's heart turns away from his or her spouse, they are gone.

It Starts As a "Fender Bender"

Several years ago, a couple in our church went through a heart-wrenching divorce. On the outside, you would have never known that anything was wrong with their marriage. They sat in church together every Sunday, and everything looked fine between them—but it wasn't.

Behind the scenes, the wife had developed an unhealthy relationship with a mutual friend of her husband. At first, the husband had no idea what was happening, but he later became suspicious. More and more, the wife began to detach emotionally from her husband as she secretly built a romantic attachment to the other man. It took months, but people eventually began to talk.

Before her husband confronted her, several of the wife's closest friends had asked her about the time she was spending with the other man. She denied any romantic interest, and broke off communication with her friends.

Finally, the husband confronted her. By this time, she was "in love" with the other man and had convinced herself that she was miserable in her marriage and had made a mistake in marrying her husband.

So, when her husband confronted her, she unloaded on him. She told him how she despised him and wanted out of the marriage. She later told him how the man with whom she was having the affair was "everything you're not."

Meanwhile, the husband had believed he and his wife were happily married and everything was fine.

Several weeks passed and then the wife moved out, leaving her husband and their four children.

It was during that time the husband went to the church for help to try to save his marriage. But in the end, his wife divorced him and married the man she had "fallen in love" with.

Emotional Distraction, Emotional or Physical Abandonment, and Adultery

Stories like this happen every day across America. Sometimes they end in divorce. Sometimes they don't. Sometimes it is the wife who gets caught up in an affair. More often it's the husband.

In the case of this couple at our church, though the husband seemed like an innocent party to his wife's adultery, he had become emotionally detached from her long before the affair. The problem actually began about a year before he suspected his wife was cheating on him. He had been given an opportunity at his job to qualify for a significant promotion for much greater income. To qualify for it, though, he buried himself in study and preparation for several months.

The good news was, he got the promotion. The bad news was, he had to spend even more time and energy applying himself to his elevated responsibilities. Consequently, he became emotionally detached from his wife and children.

Consequently, it is the failure to pursue and prioritize the relationship that begins the sure erosion of passion couples once felt for each other. And when there's a void caused by a dwindling emotional balance of what's being invested into their marriage, it's certain that something, or someone, will fill that void.

Though the man's wife was proud of him and supported him through the whole process, her emotional needs went unmet. Yet, she never complained. She actually thought it would be selfish to do so. So, she became absorbed in her children, friends and church.

By the time her attraction to the other man began, the wife was emotionally empty and had been for a long time.

Keep in mind, this couple had known the "other" man and his wife casually for several years. But then, one day, this wife and the other man crossed paths at a birthday party. As they began speaking, the first thing that sparked something in the wife was the way this guy paid attention to her.

It had been a long time since a man had looked at her attentively the way he did. He even seemed to *enjoy* talking with her. He was *interested* in what she was saying. He laughed every time she said something funny.

When the conversation was over, she thought about it for days. In fact, she began fantasizing that he was her lover.

And that's how it all began.

Emotional distraction in a marriage is a dangerous thing. Though it doesn't always lead to adultery or divorce, it always leads to problems. And it's wrong.

In this particular story, the husband whose wife left him realized after she was gone that he was a big part of the problem. Looking back, he saw how his zeal for his job had distracted him from his wife and that was the turning point in their relationship.

Like so many other marriages I see, this was a "train-wrecked" marriage that started out as a "fender bender" problem that went unnoticed, or was left ignored.

Don't Lose Sight

As I've said before, couples "fall in love" because they *focus* on each other and spend energy in pursuing one another. Then, as their relationship develops, they prioritize one another and protect their relationship from competing demands.

Consequently, it is the failure to *pursue* and *prioritize* the relationship that begins the sure erosion of passion couples once felt for each other. And when there's a void caused by a dwindling emotional balance of what's being invested into their marriage, it's certain that something, or someone, will fill that void.

As we have already seen, the greatest danger in most marriages comes from the presence of children and the promotion of careers.

For a man, it's typically a gradual turn of his attention away from his wife and toward his work or other interests outside the home.

For a woman, it's common to begin transferring more affection toward her children, or an interest such as work, in response to her husband's emotional distraction.

Either way, if you suspect you or your spouse—or both of you—are slowly being distracted from your marriage by something or someone else, here are three suggestions:

First, focus on yourself.

That's right. The fastest and easiest way to change your spouse is to change yourself. Many people make the mistake of attacking or accusing their spouses for their problems without examining their own lives, first. Jesus called it "trying to get a speck out of your brother's eye while you have a log in your own" (Matthew 7 and Luke 6).

If it's your spouse who seems distracted, ask yourself these questions:

- Have I changed the way I pursue and prioritize my wife/husband?
- Am I working as hard as I should to meet her/his needs or be romantic?
- Am I responding to her/his distraction by allowing myself to be distracted?

As you think these questions through, don't try to justify your behavior in light of your spouse's. Take responsibility for your own problems. If you realize you are doing something wrong—change it—immediately. Don't wait for your spouse to change.

A lot of marriages get into a standoff in which both spouses are waiting for the other to change first. But I like what Christian author Joyce Meyer says, "The best person does the right thing first."

So, don't focus on your spouse. Put the spotlight on yourself.

Remember, the first and most critical step in restoring the heart of a distracted spouse is to make yourself as attractive as possible to your spouse. Do for your spouse what you want done to and for you. The Bible calls it *sowing and reaping.* Sowing good seed in your spouse will result in the harvest you desire.

Next, confront your spouse in a loving manner.

After you've taken a personal inventory and dealt with your own issues, it's time to get honest with your spouse. If you feel your spouse is distracted from you, speak openly about it, but do so correctly.

Raise the issue by first affirming your love and commitment to your spouse. Then focus on how you feel, putting the spotlight on you, again, so your spouse can listen without feeling attacked and without becoming defensive.

Finally, pray.

Once you've taken responsibility for your own issues and communicated honestly, you must not try to enforce your will upon your spouse. Let the Holy Spirit be the enforcer.

If you are going to truly change the situation, you must speak the truth in love and trust God to enforce it...to change your spouse's heart. Only God can do that. If you try to do it, you will end up turning your spouse's heart from you.

Some of the greatest damage I've seen in marriages was done by well-intentioned spouses who tried to browbeat or nag a husband or wife into doing what they wanted, thinking they were on a mission from God.

So, pray and trust God for the results. That's how our marriage changed. I was a distracted, dominant husband. Yet, Karen's prayers for me led to the breakthrough in our relationship that saved our marriage.

Abandoned—But Not Without Hope

When dealing with emotional abandonment, I suggest spouses follow the counsel just given for those facing emotional distraction in their marriage.

First, put the spotlight on yourself by dealing with your own issues honestly. Then confront your spouse lovingly, and pray. All of these are powerful forces in redeeming your spouse.

To go beyond that advice, however, we have to get into some of the differences between emotional distraction and emotional, or physical, abandonment.

To begin with, when there is emotional distraction in a marriage, a couple still has some basis for communication and relationship. When there is emotional abandonment, however, there is no real communication and no real relationship. The spouse who has abandoned the marriage has basically "checked out." He or she is no longer giving into the marriage.

In cases of emotional abandonment, there's almost always a point of unresolved anger in the past, so it's good to get outside help to try and identify and resolve such issues.

If your spouse refuses to go with you to get counseling, then try intervention. Get a friend, relative or someone who has a good relationship with your spouse to talk with your spouse, getting them to address the problem. This can be done with or without your being present.

Objective input from a caring voice on the outside of your relationship can make the difference between your marriage being saved, or not.

In severe cases of emotional abandonment, or especially physical abandonment, divorce is an option. Nonetheless, it should not be entered into lightly or suddenly. In 1 Corinthians 7:10-16, the Apostle Paul has this to say about divorce:

> Now to the married I command, yet not I but the Lord: A wife is not to depart from her husband. But even if she does depart, let her remain unmarried or be reconciled to her husband. And a husband is not to divorce his wife.
>
> But to the rest I, not the Lord, say: If any brother has a wife who does not believe, and she is willing to live with him, let him not divorce her. And a woman who has a husband who does not believe, if he is willing to live with her, let her not divorce him. For the unbelieving husband is sanctified by the wife, and the unbelieving wife is sanctified by the husband; otherwise your children would be unclean, but now they are holy.
>
> But if the unbeliever departs, let him depart; a brother or a sister is not under bondage in such cases. But God has called us to peace. For how do you know, O wife, whether you will save your husband? Or how do you know, O husband, whether you will save your wife?

Addressing several issues concerning divorce, Paul begins with the common issue of a woman who is fed up with her husband and wants to leave. His command on the Lord's behalf to women in this situation is to stay in the marriage. If they choose to leave, he gives them that option, but then tells them that the only way the Lord will allow this is if they do not remarry.

When spouses are so miserable in a marriage they feel that they cannot stay, but don't have a biblical basis for divorce, they can separate or divorce as long as they do not remarry.

I almost always suggest people stay in a bad marriage because, as long as a husband and wife are together, there is a chance of a miracle happening. But when they feel they've tried everything and still have no hope, I tell them that leaving is the last option the Bible gives them, but only as long as they don't remarry. It's not an attractive scenario, but some people would rather live alone than stay in their marriages.

Dealing with the issue of abandonment, Paul then explains that if an unbelieving spouse leaves, the other is not under bondage. If a spouse truly has been abandoned, he or she is free to remarry and go on with life.

When Is It Time for Divorce?

After many years of marriage counseling, seeking God and searching the Scriptures, I believe there are several scenarios by which a person has a biblical basis for divorce.

The first is adultery.

In Matthew 19:9, Jesus said, *"Whoever divorces his wife, except for sexual immorality, and marries another, commits adultery; and whoever marries her who is divorced commits adultery."*

God does not recognize every divorce that man does. And in this text, He addressed the Pharisees who believed they could divorce their wives for any reason. He disagreed with them and told them that it was wrong unless there was sexual immorality involved.

In the Greek text, the word Jesus used for "sexual immorality" is *porneia*. It is where we get the word *pornography*. It means adultery, fornication or serious sexual deviance, such as homosexuality, incest and bestiality.

In allowing this as a reason for divorce, Jesus was not commanding us to divorce our spouses if they were unfaithful. He was just defining for the Pharisees—and us—the difference between how God views the sacredness of the marriage covenant and how people do.

Adultery and unrepentant sexual deviancy violate the marriage covenant and are sound biblical reasons for divorce.

Again, according to 1 Corinthians 7, *abandonment* is cause for divorce. And if an "unbelieving" spouse leaves, the believer is not under bondage in God's eyes.

Now, while a person may say he or she is a Christian, or in fact be one, the act of abandoning a marriage and breaking a marriage covenant is an act of unbelief. Many people get confused over this issue when their spouse abandons them, and they feel they have limited options because they were "believers." That's just it—the spouse who left obviously was not a believer. A *believer* does not just mean a person who is a "Christian." A believer is a person who is actively trusting in God. No one who abandons a spouse is trusting God. So, the person fits the label of "unbeliever."

Even if you are abandoned, that does not mean you give up easily. Every person who is abandoned should seek God and godly counseling and be careful to act with wisdom, not just react to their spouse.

I've seen many couples end up getting back together after one spouse abandoned the other. I've even seen couples reunite after years of separation or divorce.

God is a miracle-working God, and we must focus on Him in difficult times and not on our circumstances. Following Him when you've been abandoned will always bring about the best result possible, even if your marriage is not restored.

Also, if you've been abandoned, you need to be careful not to respond out of your frustrations, feelings of rejection or anger. That can simply cause more damage to the situation, as well as to any children involved.

Slow down. Turn your emotions to the Lord. Let Him heal you as you trust Him moment by moment for the strength to do the right thing. And if your spouse, who has walked out on you, does not file for divorce, then neither should you—unless, of course, the Lord is allowing you to do so.

Another opening for divorce is serious abuse or financial abandonment.

Though this is not as clearly defined in Scripture, I have sought God diligently about this issue for years as I have counseled women whose husbands would not hold down a job, or who abused them without repentance.

I do not believe a person has to leave home or commit adultery to violate the marriage covenant. I believe that serious, unrepentant abuse or the long-term unwillingness of a man to provide for his wife and children is a breach of marriage and justifies separation and divorce.

Here is what Paul says in 1 Timothy 5:8 about a man who does not provide for his family: *"But if anyone does not provide for his own, and especially for those of his household, he has denied the faith and is worse than an unbeliever."*

This does not apply to a man who struggles to hold down a job or does not make as much money as his wife wishes he did. This is the man who is chronically lazy and irresponsible. Paul says he is a notch below an unbeliever.

I believe the same is true of a man who hits a woman. There is no excuse for it.

Over the years, I have found that a physically abusive man must be dealt with in the most serious manner. Even then, many of them do not change. In those situations, I believe the man forfeits his marriage, meaning his wife is free to go on—that is, after she has tried to redeem the relationship as I described in the chapter on abuse.

Though abusive spouses may not have technically abandoned their husbands or wives, their abuse is saying in real terms that they are unwilling to live with their spouses in a civil manner. Therefore, the abused spouse is not wrong to interpret their action as abandonment. The only difference is that the victim is generally forced to leave, instead of the abusive spouse.

The sad truth is, many abusive spouses who want to end their marriages—but do not wish to lose their residence—do so by maliciously making life miserable for their spouse.

When Has It Gone Too Far?

The last area of stress in marriage that I want to examine in this chapter is adultery. Adultery is devastating to any marriage, regardless of the circumstances. And unfortunately, adultery is all too common.

While the Bible says you can divorce your spouse if he or she commits adultery, that does not mean it's God's perfect will.

The best thing I suggest you do if your spouse has committed—or is committing—adultery is to turn your feelings toward God quickly and ask

Him for the strength to do the right thing, and the ability to hear His voice in the middle of your pain and anguish.

Though there is no excuse for adultery—and you are not to blame—emotional distraction and unmet needs are a major contributor to the temptation of having an affair, as we saw earlier in this chapter.

Check yourself: Have you been meeting your spouse's needs?

Now, when it comes to the actual act of adultery, understand that there is a difference between an act of indiscretion in a moment of weakness and a *willful* act by someone who had no excuse.

If you realize *your* actions—not meeting your spouse's needs in certain areas—have contributed to the problem, take responsibility for it and keep that in mind as you consider your response to the situation.

Also, consider your spouse's attitude in the matter.

- Is your spouse being honest and open about it?
- Is your spouse broken and sorrowful?
- Was it a one-time act, or something that happened over a period of months or years?
- Did your spouse try to cover it up?

Let's say you realize your marriage was unhealthy to begin with, and your spouse's act of adultery was a short-lived event that came in a time of weakness. That's important to consider.

If that's the case and your spouse is being honest and repentant concerning it, I suggest you forgive your spouse and reconcile. Certainly, you need to get marriage counseling to help "repair" the weak areas that may have contributed to the problem and to rebuild trust.

If, however, your spouse is defiant about his or her act of

adultery...if it's still happening and he or she refuses to stop...if this is not the first time it has happened...then your response needs to be much stronger.

This is when you at least consider separation or possibly divorce. Staying in the relationship can expose you to serious disease, as well as great emotional harm.

As you do move toward divorce, I recommend you get Christian counseling to help you through the process. With your emotions frazzled, it can be a very difficult time in which to make sound decisions alone. Get some objective input.

In the end, if you and your spouse decide to try reconciling the marriage, remember that trust has to be earned.

If your spouse is repentant, make no mistake that it will take you some time to regain your trust for your husband or wife. Certainly, it's up to you to forgive your spouse and to do your part in working at the relationship. But it's up to your spouse to work at re-establishing trust in your relationship—and that takes time.

Going through the aftermath of adultery is much like grieving the death of a loved one. And whether you and your spouse reconcile or not, you need to give yourself the right to grieve. You've been through hell. Don't let anyone convince you otherwise.

In fact, not grieving properly will cause emotional problems later on. While I'm not saying you should get all depressed and dress in black, I am telling you that it's okay to cry and be sad sometimes. It's normal for you to not laugh like you may once have. It's normal not to feel like you once did.

Whatever the case, turn your pain over to God and give yourself the right to feel negative emotions as you work your way through them. In time, you will be okay.

You Were Wrong—Now What?

If it turns out that you were the spouse who committed adultery, the most important step you can take is to take responsibility for your actions and the gravity of what you have done.

Regardless of what you have done to hurt your marriage or your spouse, you have sinned against God and broken one of the Ten Commandments. So, begin by repenting to God and to your spouse and to anyone else who may have been damaged by your behavior, such as your children.

Repentance is to not blame what you did on your spouse or someone else. Repentance is to do whatever is necessary to make the relationship right.

Now, if you truly repent to God, He will forgive you—but that does not mean there will not be any consequences for your behavior.

Submitting to the counsel and accountability of a pastor, spiritual leader or Christian counselor is vitally important because you got into your problems by being secretive and doing things on your own. The only way you're going to solve your problems is to bring your heart out into the light and become accountable and submitted.

Encourage but do not try to force your spouse to go for counseling. Let your spouse know that you are going because you love him or her and want your marriage to work—not so you can try to get your spouse fixed or put the spotlight on his or her problems.

If your marriage lasts, you will have to prove you have changed. Trust can be lost in a moment of sin or foolishness, but it can only be gained over time. So, be patient with your spouse. Do not demand immediate trust from your spouse or blame your spouse for being mistrustful or suspicious of you for a while. If you truly want your spouse to trust you, do not be demanding with your words. Earn the trust with your life. Trust can be restored.

Finally, break off any contact from the person, or persons, with whom you have committed adultery, even if it requires your changing jobs, or moving. Be wise, and do not lie to yourself about the relationship.

Furthermore, do not have a close friend in someone who is adulterous or sympathetic toward adultery.

I've noticed over the years that adultery and divorce run in groups.

Instead, get involved in a good church and develop relationships with people who are committed to God and their marriages, as well.

I have dealt with many difficult counseling situations over the years. But I have never seen a situation, no matter how complex or devastating, that God could not handle, or where He withdrew His love.

Whatever you may be facing, turn to Him as you face it—because nothing is impossible with God, and He always works on the side of the person who is trying to save a marriage and do the right thing.

Chapter Thirteen

Resolving the Stress of
An Unequally Yoked Marriage

We are commanded by God not to be "unequally yoked" with unbelievers. Specifically, we are told, *"Do not be unequally yoked together with unbelievers. For what fellowship has righteousness with lawlessness?"* (2 Corinthians 6:14).

In this passage, the word *yoke* can mean two things.

First, it can mean a piece of wood used to bond animals together, such as oxen, to perform a task.

Second, it can mean a pair of scales, such as those used in Biblical times to weigh produce or money.

When relating this principle to being unequally yoked in marriage, I believe both definitions can apply.

To be unequally yoked means that an intimate and binding relationship is developed with a person who has significantly different values than your own. Marriage is the most intimate and binding relationship on earth. For that reason, you must be careful to enter into it with a person who shares your values and uses the same "scales" to weigh decisions.

According to Genesis 2, God is to be the force that binds couples together in marriage. We could say that He is their yoke. And to that, Jesus would add, *"What God has joined together, let not man separate"* (Matthew 19:6).

Getting the Short End of the Yoke

There are three categories of people who find themselves unequally yoked in marriage.

The first category includes people who knowingly married a person who was not a Christian. Whether it was out of ignorance or malice, they made a mistake in doing so and will usually realize it later on when problems develop.

I have known many Christian people over the years who practice what I call "missionary dating." They purposely date people who are not Christians with the intention of getting them born again, either before they get married, or after.

Needless to say, I have seen a lot of pain and heartache produced by this attitude.

It's perfectly normal for an individual to be attracted to a person, whether or not that person is a Christian. After all, attraction is not based on beliefs.

Furthermore, it is perfectly fine to develop a friendship with a non-believer of the opposite sex. If the friendship is to become anything more than a friendship, it's up to the believer to let the non-Christian "friend" know that the relationship can go no further because of the requirements of the believer's faith.

On many occasions, that alone is enough to end the relationship. Sometimes, however, the unbeliever will express a desire to become a Christian, as well as pursue the relationship. That's wonderful if there's fruit indicating that their conversion was real—and not just for the sake of the relationship. A person's faith needs to be expressed long enough before marriage to prove that it's real, as well as mature enough to withstand the tests of married life.

The second category is made up of people who thought they were marrying Christians, but later found out differently, or their spouses changed significantly.

That's why I believe so strongly in good counseling—before marriage—in which issues like this are discussed and couples find out the ways they will agree and disagree before they are married. It helps avoid the surprise of finding out after they're married that they actually have little to nothing in common pertaining to religious beliefs, practices in tithing and giving, their desire to serve God, and so on.

The third category of people who are unequally yoked are those who were not believers when they married, but were saved afterward and their spouse wasn't.

Now, closely related to this third group are the people who often feel like they are unequally yoked, but they are not. These are those zealous people who are married and have a deep love for God, yet their Christian spouses do not share their same level of passion or commitment to the things of God. Maybe their spouse is immature, sinful or absorbed in other interests. Whatever the reason, they know there is an imbalance of zeal for God. If that describes you in your marriage, I believe you will find some help in this chapter, as well.

First Things First

If you find yourself in one of these categories of spouses married to someone who is not a believer, first, I want to encourage you that—while you may be unequally yoked with an earthly partner—you are not alone. Almighty God is right there with you.

Indeed, you are yoked with a heavenly partner—and that makes a world of difference.

Now, in the meantime, while you may be believing God for your spouse to come into the kingdom, I also want to encourage you with six practical steps that can get you through to the other side of this situation.

First, as you have probably figured out by now, I am big on repenting. And why not? James 4:6-10 promises us this:

> God resists the proud, but gives grace to the humble. Therefore submit to God. Resist the devil and he will flee from you. Draw near to God and He will draw near to you. Cleanse your hands, you sinners; and purify your hearts, you double-minded. Lament and mourn and weep! Let your laughter be turned to mourning and your joy to gloom. Humble yourselves in the sight of the Lord, and He will lift you up.

Who couldn't use a little lifting up by God?

Who couldn't stand to have some devils fleeing?

And who couldn't do better by having God draw near?

Well, to get there you have to start with the "humble yourself" part...and the "submit to God" part.

Why?

Because, quite simply, God resists the proud. That literally means He strongly sets Himself in opposition to pride, wherever He finds it. In other words, when we're walking in pride, the devil is the least of our problems because we're fighting against God.

So, my "step one" is simply this:

Repent to God for any mistakes in your past, or sins that are in your life at this moment. As I said earlier, some people are in unequally yoked marriages because of rebellion to God. They knew they were marrying unbelievers, and they knew God's Word said not to do it.

If that describes you, then recognize your sin and repent of it. Don't mess around with it—get rid of it.

Now, the reason I make this point about repentance first is because you're not going to make any progress in your situation unless God is on your side. And to get Him there, humility and submission are essential.

So, realize you have sinned, then, repent to God and receive His forgiveness. Remember, He *will* exalt you.

Stay in for the Long Haul

The second step you need to take as a believer married to an unbeliever is to commit fully—whole-heartedly—to your marriage.

We saw earlier in 1 Corinthians 7:10-16, what the Apostle Paul told believers who were married to unbelievers—he basically gave clear instructions for them to commit to their marriages.

But sadly enough, I have counseled many people who, even when their non-Christian spouses wanted to stay in the marriage, have turned their hearts away from their spouses or left them. They did this despite being the very ones who complained about the condition of their marriages and the fact that their spouses were unbelievers.

As a believer, you are supposed to be a reflection of Christ's love and character. And it was His love that, in spite of your sin, drew you to Him. His grace is the most powerful force on this earth.

Therefore, as the believing spouse, you have the best chance of anyone in the world of demonstrating Christ's love to your husband or wife and leading him or her to an understanding and love of the Lord. This must become the focus and standard of your behavior.

So, no matter what your spouse is or is not doing, commit yourself to redeeming him or her by the love of Christ. Even if you are disgusted and feel like your spouse is your enemy, Jesus has told you to love your enemies.

Committing to your marriage also means that you energetically love and pursue your spouse as you meet his or her needs. In other words, make your marriage a priority and pursue your spouse. It's a huge mistake to become passive toward your marriage as your spouse sees you spending your energies on spiritual pursuits.

As the believing spouse, you have the best chance of anyone in the world of demonstrating Christ's love to your husband or wife and leading him or her to an understanding and love of the Lord.

Certainly, you need to give God top priority and pursue Him. But that does not exempt you from loving your spouse.

Realize that there is a difference between your commitment to God and your commitment to church and other Christian interests.

I'm a pastor. You can imagine how important I think church is. But church is not more important than your marriage. God is more important than your marriage—your personal relationship with Him through prayer, Bible reading, and a daily walk with Him. But church and other things are not as important.

I advise people in unequally yoked marriages to pursue their relationship with God, whether their spouses condone it or not. I also counsel them to go to church at least once a week, whether their spouses approve or go with them.

I do caution people, however, not to express their faith in a self-righteous way, or make their spouse feel replaced by God or church pursuits.

Unsaved spouses can grow to resent God and church because they see them as the two elements that busted their marriage and took their spouses from them.

As you love your spouse aggressively and practice your faith respectfully, you have the best chance of building your marriage and breaking through your spouse's spiritual hardness.

While you shouldn't apologize for your faith or allow your unsaved spouse to keep you from the essential pursuits and practices that keep you spiritually healthy, don't turn your heart away from your spouse, either.

Love your spouse and demonstrate that being a Christian makes you better and blesses his or her life as a result. Let your spouse receive the overflow of God's love coming out of you as you turn your heart toward him or her.

Pretend You're Married to Jesus

We have already covered the issue of submission described by the Apostle Paul in Ephesians 5. What I want to focus on at this point is the issue of submitting with an attitude of honor, which Paul explains in verses 22-24:

"Wives, submit to your own husbands, as to the Lord. For the husband is head of the wife, as also Christ is head of the church; and He is the Savior of the body. Therefore, just as the church is subject to Christ, so let the wives be to their own husbands in everything."

Many wives, even those who are *equally* yoked, have a major problem when it comes to submitting to their husbands "as to the Lord." They view this instruction as demeaning. And since their husbands' character is far from that of Christ's, they excuse themselves from compliance to this command.

When a woman understands the real meaning of the command to honor and submit to her husband, however, it helps her to see the wisdom behind it.

Honor is a man's primary need. We've already studied that. It's true of every man—saved and unsaved.

The Bible tells women to carry an attitude of honor toward their husbands, like they would toward Christ, because it is a man's greatest need—and it's what attracts a man to a woman.

Ladies, honor is the key to your husband's heart. When you treat Him with an attitude of careful respect and honor, it meets his greatest need in life.

There are two main problems, though, that women must overcome in honoring their husbands as they should.

The first problem is Satan, the Accuser. The devil's job is to get all of us to focus on each other's faults. This is especially true in marriage. He wants us to focus on what is wrong with our spouses, so we will resent and reject them.

Mess up the devil's day and focus on what's right with your husband, for a change, and treat him with an attitude of honor.

Certainly, you are your husband's equal and you have every right to speak your mind and carry an equal weight in the decisions of the home. But the spirit you carry toward your husband still must be one of honor.

The second problem women must overcome in honoring their husbands is pride. This is especially true in unequally yoked marriages.

When I first began in marriage counseling, I helped many women who were unequally yoked in their marriages. After a while, I saw a pattern that shocked me. I actually noticed that many women who had unsaved husbands left them after their husbands were saved.

In other words, they reacted negatively to their husbands' getting saved, even after saying to me and others that they wanted their husbands saved more than anything.

The reason a wife might respond negatively when her husband is born again or begins to change for the better is because she is emotionally unhealthy, having low self-esteem. Though she complained about her husband's problems, she actually married him that way because it made her feel better about herself and more secure in the relationship.

Therefore, the better the husband gets, the more it puts the spotlight on the wife's problems. Before long, she will either have to address her problems or leave the relationship to find another "sick" man to marry.

Then there's the pride.

As long as her husband was an unbeliever, the born-again wife was the spiritual leader in the home. As one woman told me about her newly saved husband, "He's a baby Christian, so I'm not going to listen to him!"

If you are telling yourself that you cannot honor your husband because he is unsaved, or has too many problems—but things will change once he gets saved—you are not being honest with yourself.

But if you can honor your husband and carry a spirit of submission toward him now, you can easily do it when he is saved and has changed for the better.

The Fear Factor

I admire women. They're highly relational and naturally spiritual. If it weren't for women, the world would be in a much bigger mess than it is today—and so would all of us men.

In spite of all their strengths in relationships and marriage, however, I often see a common weakness in women that affects their marriages and relationships negatively—fear.

The blessing of women is that they are so in tune with their emotions. Yet, Satan does everything he can to take those strengths of women and exploit them. Fear is his primary weapon to do that...just as he did with Eve in the Garden of Eden.

Satan is so good at this that he convinced a woman who had a perfect body, a perfect husband, and who lived in a perfect paradise that she was being abused.

And, out of fear, she fell for it...sinned...and lost it all. If the devil could do all that in a perfect environment, he can certainly do it with any of us unless we expose and defeat him.

Responding to fear and negative emotions is a woman's greatest problem in marriage. This is especially true when her husband is unsaved or sinful.

Regarding this point, the Apostle Peter has specific instructions for women whose husbands do not obey the word:

Wives, likewise, be submissive to your own husbands, that even if some do not obey the word, they, without a word, may be won by the conduct of their wives, when they observe your chaste conduct accompanied by fear. Do not let your adornment be merely outward—arranging the hair, wearing gold, or putting on fine apparel—rather let it be the hidden person of the heart, with the incorruptible beauty of a gentle and quiet spirit, which is very precious in the sight of God. For in this manner, in former times, the holy women who trusted in God also adorned themselves, being submissive to their

> own husbands, as Sarah obeyed Abraham, calling him lord, whose daughters you are <u>if you do good and are not afraid with any terror</u> (1 Peter 3:1-6).

Peter is speaking to women in many situations. Some are in unequally yoked marriages, while others are married to believers who are disobedient to God in one or more areas.

The truth is, all women will have to endure the mistakes and sins of their husbands. But Peter is telling them to do it with a righteous response, and with a respectful attitude—believing God will use their good example to change their husbands.

After going into quite a bit of detail about how a wife can literally change her husband "without a word," he tells wives that they can succeed if they will act in faith and "are not afraid with any terror."

Again, Peter knew that Satan uses fear against women to keep them from obeying God and acting in faith.

Then, Peter mentions Sarah's faith to the women he is trying to call to a higher standard. Oftentimes, we forget that on two occasions, Sarah's husband, Abraham, lied about her being his sister instead of his wife, and she was taken in as a foreign king's wife to sleep with him. Only by God's grace was she rescued each time.

- **Faith focuses on how big God is – fear focuses on how big the problem is.**
- **Faith is dependent upon God to act – fear is dependent upon you to act.**
- **Faith is able to love even in the worst circumstances – fear can take the best circumstances and mess them up.**

I know your husband makes mistakes, but he probably hasn't done anything that bad. That is Peter's point in bringing up Sarah's faith and the issue of fear. He's telling women, "Hey, if Sarah could do it, you can do it. God came through for her...He will come through for you if you put your faith in Him and don't respond in fear!"

I'm sure Sarah felt a great deal of fear on both occasions when Abraham lied and she was taken away from him.

Can you imagine what that would have been like?

But regardless of what she felt, Sarah responded in faith.

By no means is it a sin to feel fear, or anything else. It is a sin to be controlled by your feelings and not by faith in God.

In 2 Timothy 1:7, we find that *"God has not given us a spirit of fear, but of power and of love and of a sound mind."*

Notice that Paul refers to fear as a "spirit." Not only do I believe that almost all destructive fear is demonic in nature, but I also believe it is actually a spirit of false prophecy.

What I'm referring to is when you are going through difficulties, like in marriage, and the devil uses this to send a demonic spirit of fear to you to tell you what is going to happen if you don't act in a certain way.

An example is a couple who is having money problems.

A spirit of fear uses the anxiety over the money problems to whisper to the wife's spirit, "Hey, if you don't do something now, he's going to break the family."

The spirit of fear then gives a flash-forward into the future for the woman to see in her imagination. She sees a picture of humiliation and poverty. When she sees it, fear strikes her heart and if she responds to it, she will sin—all the while believing she is doing something she "has" to do.

You see, fear is the opposite of faith. Faith tells you to do one thing, and fear tells you another.

Faith focuses on how big God is—fear focuses on how big the problem is.

Faith is dependent upon God to act—fear is dependent upon you to act.

Faith is able to love even in the worst circumstances—fear can take the best circumstances and mess them up.

It's your choice. You can be a faith-filled woman of God who faces the storms of life and your husband's problems with a confident spirit that is "very precious" to God. Or, you can react to your circumstances by allowing your fears and frustrations to dictate your behavior.

> **You can either be a faith-filled woman of God who faces the storms of life and your husband's problems with a confident spirit that is "very precious" to God. Or, you can react to your circumstances by allowing your fears and frustrations to dictate your behavior.**

God is looking for some good Sarahs. He's calling godly women out of the world's way of thinking to focus on the beauty of their spirit and not just of their flesh.

If you respond to His call to a life of faith, God will reward you and fulfill His promises to you. That is an important key in becoming God's partner to change your marriage and to save your husband.

When Children Come Into Play

One of the most volatile issues regarding an unequally yoked marriage is the spiritual training and influence of the children. In some cases, an unsaved spouse is passive or even supportive of the fact that the saved spouse takes the children to church or trains them to actively practice the Christian faith.

If that's your case, it's a blessing. At least there is no opposition to your ability to influence your children spiritually.

When you have a degree of liberty with the children, do everything possible to raise them with Bible knowledge, church involvement, and your example of practicing the faith on a daily basis and training them to do the same.

In all of this, honor your unsaved spouse. Tell your spouse what you're doing, and ask for his or her blessing. As long as your relationship with each other is healthy and your spouse does not see what you are doing as negative toward him or her, it probably will not be an issue.

In fact, it's common in unequally yoked marriages for the saved spouses to resent the fact that they are working alone to raise the children with spiritual values and beliefs.

Having already addressed the issue of honoring your spouse and not allowing your emotions to dictate your responses, remember that your children need to see you respecting their other parent, too.

Therefore, as the children start asking questions about why Dad is not a Christian, or why Mom doesn't go to church, you must be careful not to put your spouse down or speak with contempt.

You can be honest about your spiritual differences without creating division or anxiety. The spirit in which you talk about your spouse to your children, or talk to your spouse in front of them, is critical.

Just as with any other parents, unequally yoked spouses need to be careful to disagree and decide on issues concerning their children behind closed doors. It creates great stress for children to hear their parents fight or bicker.

If something happens in a family situation that violates or concerns you, wait until you are alone with your spouse to talk about it. That's best for your marriage and for your children. While it's not likely you and your spouse can come to perfect agreement on every issue, strive to present a mutually honoring and united front to your children.

Now, when you're in a situation where the unbelieving spouse is hostile toward your faith, do everything possible to communicate and agree with your spouse in private. If there is a breakdown in communication and your spouse persists in bashing Christianity openly in front of the children, or encourages the children in sinful or destructive behavior, you need to treat that seriously.

To begin with, seek the Lord. Be careful to follow Him—and not your feelings. Pray and ask for His guidance. Ask Him for the grace and wisdom you need to do the right thing. Also, get counsel from a godly friend or pastor. Ask for help to make the right decisions.

I believe that once a spouse becomes destructive, he or she has crossed a line. A difference in beliefs is one thing, but destructive behavior is another.

An example of this kind of destructive behavior would be a spouse who brings illegal drugs into the home, allows the children to drink alcohol, buys them liquor, or views pornography openly, maybe making it available to the children—these are all serious issues that require serious attention.

In these types of situations, it is appropriate to give a clear ultimatum to an unhealthy spouse to let him or her know you will not tolerate destructive influences in the home. Let your spouse know—in love—that if the behavior continues, a separation will become necessary.

Of course, in situations like this you would definitely want custody of the children.

If you do end up separating, you still need to communicate your commitment to the marriage and love for your spouse, but with an unyielding insistence for real change.

If your spouse does change, you can reconcile.

If your spouse does not change, you need to decide when to go on with your life.

As you go through the process of dealing with a destructive spouse, make sure you talk with your children in an open manner. Tell them what's going on and why you are doing what you are doing. Tell them that though you believe the other parent is wrong, you still love the parent and are praying for him or her.

Be up front with your children, letting them know your actions are motivated out of love and concern for them and your spouse, and not out of spitefulness or revenge. Keep your focus on God and use this as a teaching opportunity for your children of how to trust in God and love hurtful people in difficult times.

It's wrong to allow children to be harmed by a spouse who is destructive. If your spouse loves you and wants to make the marriage work, he or she will change and respect your desires. If your spouse refuses to change, then that is a danger sign and it necessitates serious action.

Don't Do It Alone

When it comes to facing the stress of an unequally yoked marriage, you can count on the people around you to always do one of three things—either they will help you succeed, not help you at all, or encourage you to do the wrong thing.

Quite honestly, this is a time like no other when you find out who is your *real* family. And this is a time like no other to have that "real" family gathered around you, supporting in every means possible.

That's why I highly suggest having a support group of godly friends to pray with you and encourage you.

Even the strongest believer cannot survive alone. Satan is like a hungry wolf, preying on the sheep wandering away from the flock.

Besides, if you are married to an unbeliever, your need for spiritual support cannot be fulfilled at home. That, in turn, makes the quality of the other relationships in your life even more important.

If you work outside of your home, you are probably faced with people at work who would encourage you to divorce or to do the "wrong thing." Granted, you cannot always choose the people you work with, but you can choose your friends and those you relate to closely. When you seek them out, you will find people who share your values and are committed to God. These are the kinds of people you need around you.

The best place to find these people is in a strong, Bible-believing church. Get involved and build relationships with people who will pray with you and encourage you.

It only takes two believers gathered together in prayer to claim God's greatest promises and enjoy His most intimate presence.

Now, that's not a license to go around telling everyone your problems. But you should find a few people you trust who can listen to you, pray with you, and keep you accountable to do the right thing.

God works in an atmosphere of faith and godly fellowship. Jesus explained how in Matthew 18:19-20:

"Again I say to you that if two of you agree on earth concerning anything that they ask, it will be done for them by My Father in heaven. For where two or three are gathered together in My name, I am there in the midst of them."

It only takes two believers gathered together in prayer to claim God's greatest promises and enjoy His most intimate presence.

The power of prayer and righteous fellowship cannot be overstated or underestimated. If you do not have one already, find a prayer partner you can meet with regularly and shake the gates of heaven together in prayer until you receive the marriage miracle you desire.

I pastor a church of about 7,000 people. And I have many couples in my congregation who came from unequally yoked backgrounds. But, today, their marriages are whole. Their families are whole.

Why?

Because they both worship and serve God together, now. In almost every case, it was the righteous and faith-filled actions of the believing spouse that led his or her mate to Christ. Now, not only are they receiving a reward in this life for their sacrifice, but it will be even greater in eternity.

So, don't get discouraged. Put your faith in God and follow Him. He loves you and desires to work through you to do miracles in your marriage, today.

Notes

Chapter 4
John M. Gottman, Ph.D., *The Seven Principles for Making Marriage Work*, ©1999 Crown Publishing Group, Random House.

Chapter 5
Kenneth O. Doyle, *The Social Meaning of Money and Property: In Search of a Talisman*, ©1999 SAGE Publications, p. 43-44.

Chapter 6
JAMA, *Journal of the American Medical Association*, ©1999, p. 73.

Chapter 9
Willard F. Harley, Jr., *His Needs, Her Needs: Building an Affair-Proof Marriage*, ©2001 Baker Books.

Chapter 11
Linda J. Waite and Maggie Gallagher, *The Case for Marriage: Why Married People are Happier, Healthier, and Better Off Financially*, ©2000 Doubleday, Random House.

Judith S. Wallerstein, Julia M. Lewis and Sandra Blakeslee, *The Unexpected Legacy of Divorce: A 25 Year Landmark Study*, ©2000 Hyperion Press.

859.4086

6463179224